Gender and Diversity in Management

Gender and Diversity in Management

A Concise Introduction

Caroline Gatrell and Elaine Swan

Los Angeles • London • New Delhi • Singapore

First published 2008

SAGE Publications Ltd
1 Oliver's Yard
55 City Road
London EC1Y 1SP

SAGE Publications Inc.
2455 Teller Road
Thousand Oaks, California 91320

SAGE Publications India Pvt Ltd
B 1/I 1 Mohan Cooperative Industrial Area
Mathura Road
New Delhi 110 044

SAGE Publications Asia-Pacific Pte Ltd
33 Pekin Street #02-01
Far East Square
Singapore 048763

Library of Congress Control Number: 2007936092

British Library Cataloguing in Publication data

A catalogue record for this book is available from
the British Library

ISBN 978-1-4129-2823-6
ISBN 978-1-4129-2824-3 (pbk)

Typeset by C&M Digital (P) Ltd, Chennai, India
Printed in India by Replika Press Pvt. Ltd
Printed on paper from sustainable resources

CG
For Tony, and Pam and Max

ES
For everyone involved, past and present, in the Institute of
Women's Studies Lancaster University

CONTENTS

ACKNOWLEDGEMENTS

We would like to acknowledge all in the PhD Pressure Group for their support and friendship over many years. In relation to this project, we would like especially to thank Dr Ellie Hamilton and Dr Valerie Stead. We also wish to recognise the support of our colleagues in the Gender in Management Special Interest Group, acknowledging the work of Adelina Broadbridge in establishing and chairing the group, and with particular thanks to Professor Beverly Metcalfe. We would also both wish to recognise the contribution made by our students to this text – we continually learn from those we teach, in relation both to research and management practices.

Elaine wishes, in particular, to thank Professor Sara Ahmed for her inspirational work and friendship, and Dr Shona Hunter for her critical thinking and friendship. Caroline would also like to thank Dr Imogen Tyler for all her support both as friend and colleague. We would also like to thank our partners Steve Fox (Elaine) and Tony Gatrell (Caroline) for their support and encouragement over many years.

WHAT DO WE MEAN BY GENDER AND DIVERSITY IN MANAGEMENT?

> All organizations have inequality regimes, defined as loosely interrelated practices, processes, actions, and meanings that result in and maintain class, gender, and racial inequalities within particular organizations. (Joan Acker 2006: 443)

Introduction

In the past thirty years, the literature on women and men in management, on diversity in management, and what Acker terms 'inequality regimes' has grown (see, for example, Halford and Leonard 2001; Maddock 1999; Alvesson and Due Billing 1997; Prasad et al. 1997; Mills and Tancred 1992). Changes to legislation and policy have focused on equality of opportunity and diversity, meaning that, *in theory*, the possibilities of careers in management should be open to everyone, regardless of their gender and/or ethnic background. So why do we need a book entitled *Gender and Diversity in Management*? A quick analysis of the gender and the cultural backgrounds of board-level managers within many public and private sector organisations will rapidly demonstrate that the top positions in business, and in the public sector in the UK, are largely filled by white, able-bodied men. Furthermore, studies by government agencies such as the Equal Opportunities Commission (EOC 2005a), research by academics (Ahmed et al. 2006), and surveys utilised by activists such as the Gay Rights group Stonewall (TUC 1999) show that discrimination within the workplace remains widespread and persistent and leads to further inequalities in a broader context. Thus, legislation and policy notwithstanding, 'minoritised' groups (by which we mean social groups who are actively constructed as 'other' or outside the dominant norm) continue to face oppression and unequal treatment at work through inequality regimes. The forms of inequality, discrimination and oppression in the workplace can vary but include:

> **systematic disparities between participants in power and control over goals, resources, and outcomes; workplace decisions such as how to organize work; opportunities for promotion and interesting work; security in employment and benefits; pay and other monetary rewards; respect; and pleasures in work and work relations. (Acker 2006: 443)**

Oppression can also refer to symbolic and actual violence.

Women from a range of social locations are still held back by the existence of a wide range of formal and informal organisational practices and processes, often referred to as the 'glass ceiling', and each year tens of thousands of women face pregnancy-related discrimination at work. In terms of career advancement, black and minority ethnic workers experience what is called a 'concrete ceiling', and are often pushed by employers into roles which give them responsibility for diversity in their workplace, but which are not recognised when it comes to promotion or recognition. They thus experience a range of racisms (Ahmed et al. 2006). Workers with disabilities may be seen as a 'problem' by employers who are reluctant to make 'reasonable adjustments' in the workplace so as to offer workers with disabilities a workplace that is less disabling (Disability Rights Commission *c*. 2004). And gay men, lesbians, bisexuals and transgendered employees face discrimination, and even abuse, in their daily working lives (TUC 1999).

Glossing some complex debates, we can say, in sum, that there is a disparity between the ideals espoused in policies and in theory and what is actually happening in practice. Furthermore, while there continues to be a growing level of scholarly interest in the field(s) of gender and diversity in management, there are still many debates from which the notions of gender and diversity are excluded. Thus, for example, so-called 'mainstream' discussions about 'strategy', 'power', 'economy' and 'knowledge' are often played out in management or organisational journals and books without any reference either to gender or to race, sexuality, or disability, as if these organisational concepts and practices are somehow neutral when, arguably, the reverse is true. Organisations themselves tend to be constructed as gender-free, colour blind or asexual. In examining processes of inequality in organisations, we can help improve workplace practices but also enhance management and organisational theorising by opening up what has been a partial view of workplace life. Influential feminist organisational theorists see this as a radical move which will produce a new account of organisational life.

The purpose of this mini-guide is twofold. Our main aim is to provide an accessible introduction to gender, race, sexuality and disability, and diversity in management. Our main focus is on waged work and employment, rather than unpaid labour that women do in the home or community. As such, we cover contemporary issues which are central to the debate among scholars and practitioners. At the same time, however, while attempting to present these topics in a straightforward manner, we attempt to set in context the various debates around gender and diversity in management. Even the terms 'gender' and 'diversity' are highly contested and examined from quite different perspectives, which we introduce in the following chapters. *Gender and Diversity in Management* is designed for students on courses across a range of business and management subjects, including women in management, gender in management, equal opportunities and diversity, and human resource management. We also hope it will be valuable to managers from a range of organisations and sectors who wish to understand better the debates around gender and diversity in management, or who seek a practical and up-to-date guide to contemporary thought and practice.

It would be impossible, in one mini-guide (or even in a heavyweight textbook), to cover issues of gender and diversity across the globe. For this reason, our main point of reference is the UK. However, although localised and legislative differences mean that there are different cultural perspectives on gender, diversity and management, many of the concepts and practices outlined here are of international relevance. Thus, although many of the examples given in this book are from the UK, the ideas and theoretical perspectives may be applied to a wider context, albeit reconfigured to take account of national and cultural perspectives and political contexts. Before we proceed, we will briefly define how we are using the core concepts of 'gender' and 'diversity'.

What Do We Mean by 'Gender'?

The term 'gender', although widely used in everyday discourse, policy documents and academic literature, is hotly debated. There is no one definition that works across all contexts or that is used by all theorists or activists. As leading organisational theorist Joan Acker writes, 'although the term [gender] is widely used, there is no common understanding of its meaning, even amongst feminist scholars' (1992: 565). Gender, then, is not self-evident or unproblematic but has immense consequences for the way that the workplace and life outside the workplace are organised and experienced (Wharton 2005). Gender not only organises bodies but bifurcates the whole social world into segregated domains in the workplace, in cultural practices and in the home. In spite of many differences, contemporary gender theorists and activists tend to move away from understanding gender as a natural, unchanging or even biological essence (sometimes referred to as 'essentialism'). For most social theorists, gender is a social construction. This means that gender – and, in fact, other social categories, such as race, sexuality and disability – are seen as the result of human social processes, actions, language, thought and practices. There are many debates on what it means to say that something is socially constructed. For our purposes, we can say that it emphasises the ongoing and dynamic processes and mechanisms through which gender, race, sexuality and disability are brought into being in the workplace.

To stress the ongoing production of gender, race, sexuality and disability, many social theorists also refer to verbs: for example, gendering, racialising, or disabling. This use of the participle attempts to get at the way that gender, race, etc. are not simply pre-existing as one enters the workplace. Rather than seeing gender, race, etc. as an individual's properties, they are understood as outcomes of social practices and as being continuously produced and reproduced outside the workplace but also through workplace structures, discourses, cultures, practices, policies, interactions and procedures. Gender and other social differences are thus seen as processes rather than as given traits or essences: thus, gender is actively produced in and through the workplace, and does not simply exist as something that is static prior to or outside the workplace.

There are still debates among activists, feminists, critical race theorists and organisational theorists on which of the above is the most salient practice through which gender and gendering are reproduced. One useful summary model comes from sociologist, Amy Wharton (2005). She suggests that there are three main levels at which theorists suggest gendering can operate. First, it operates at the level of individualised processes or practices, such as socialisation, psychological factors, and/or personal preferences. Thus, it might be imagined that women are more co-operative and nurturing than men, and men more aggressive and individualistic than women. Secondly, gender and gendering are seen to operate at the level of social interactions. For example, influential ethnomethodologists, West and Zimmerman (1987: 127), suggest that gender is the 'activity of managing situated conduct in the light of normative conceptions of attitudes and activities appropriate for one's sex category' and emphasise that it is 'not a set of traits, nor a variable, nor a role, but the product of social doings' (1987: 129). They focus on the way that social interaction is a means to 'do' gender. Finally, Wharton argues that for other activists and academics, gender, gendering and gendered inequalities are reproduced through social practices, structures, processes, cultures of organisations and institutions.

These ways of understanding gender move away from individualistic or interactional models: gender is not an individual possession but is created and reproduced through cultures, practices and structures (Wharton 2005). For example, Joan Acker (1990) argues that organisational structure is not gender-neutral and that assumptions about gender underline organisational contracts, documents, hierarchies and job descriptions. While each is partial, these different perspectives point to the complexity of gender and also the different types of intervention needed to address regimes of inequality (Acker 2006; Wharton 2005).

These different views on gender in the workplace lead to an ongoing debate about whether a theoretical and a practical focus should be on gender in management, rather than on women in management. The idea of 'gender and gendering' as opposed to 'women' in management as an analytic lens means that the relationality between men and women, masculinity and femininity – the way that they cannot be thought apart from each other – can be emphasised. The notion of gender and gendering also draws attention to the social construction of masculinity and femininity: the active practices through which they are reproduced in the workplace in different ways (Kerfoot and Knights 1996; Wajcman 1998). Some have argued that the term 'women in management' can reinforce notions of biological or cultural essentialism – the idea that all women are alike and have the same political interests. It is also deemed to focus on women as individuals, or a social group, rather than on management or organisational processes. In contrast, it has also been argued that in erasing the term 'women' the notion of gender threatens to dilute the achievements of first- and second-wave feminists. For example, the question has been raised whether the concept of gender 'undoes the accomplishments of the past thirty-five years in bringing women and women's standpoints to the forefront in research knowledge and cultural production' (Davis et al. 2006: 2). The concept and politics of gender in the workplace is still contested and these debates are reflected in the following chapters.

What Do We Mean by 'Diversity'?

Having discussed the concept of gender, we now turn to 'diversity'. Diversity is a fascinating notion in relation to management and the workplace. For one thing, it is a very ill-defined and slippery term. In this book, we use it in two main ways. First, we consider diversity in relation to management practices to deal with the changing demographic of employees and customers, and inequalities in the workplace. Thus, in Chapter 4, we explain how 'equal opportunities' polices have, in many cases, been superseded by notions of diversity. For some, the notion of 'diversity' is seen as more inclusive than the idea of equal opportunities. The second way that we use it is to bring other social categories into discussions of management and the workplace. This second notion of diversity allows us, in Chapter 5, to explore in some detail the disadvantage and oppressive treatment faced by a range of social groups. We consider, for example, the problems faced by those who are gay, lesbian or bisexual, in relation to management. We suggest that, while some aspects of social policy and legislation may *appear* to offer equality of treatment (for example, enabling gay couples to become civil partners, with similar rights to married heterosexual couples), the experience of some gay employees is one of social exclusion and of being expected, at work, to comply with heterosexual 'norms'. Thus, while, on the surface, the situation of gay managers might seem improved, in practice life in the workplace may appear to have changed very little – this presumably motivating the Gay Rights group 'Stonewall' to observe in their present advertising campaign: 'It's 2007 – not 1977'. In relation to black and minority ethnic staff, we discuss organisational processes of racialisation and racism, and the different ways these are understood by activists and academics. Once again, we are emphasising sexuality, race and disability as social constructions, the products of active, dynamic workplace and socio-cultural practices and not biological or natural essences.

The book is presented in two sections, 'gender' and 'diversity'. This is not because we see the two issues as somehow separate. In fact, as many theorists argue, social categories need to be understood as 'mutually reinforcing or contradicting processes' (Acker 2006: 443). As black feminists and lesbian activists have pointed out, there are immense problems in assuming an undifferentiated and universal category of 'woman'. Sometimes referred to as *inter-sectionality*, social categories of race, gender, sexuality, disability, age and class are understood as interrelating and mutually constituting. Analytically, these distinct social markers of differences are understood as both interconnected *and* as separate and specific. In this book, we separate them out for analytic purposes. This is partly because the debates, histories and forms of discrimination and oppression are in some respects different, and partly to emphasise issues to do with race, sexuality and disability in the workplace, as these are often ignored in much organisational and management theory.

We do not deal with class or age in any depth as this is a concise introduction and we could not cover all areas: class has been covered in some detail in organisational theory and age now needs to be thought about in relation to the very recent legislation. Throughout the book we have tried to emphasise the importance of the way that minoritised groups have developed significant individual and collective coping strategies to deal with persistent disadvantage and oppression. We thus consider struggles and political activism among disadvantaged groups, to demand and influence change. We also point to the way that activists and academics have been debating the role of social groups in society, and in relation to employment, for over a hundred years. There have been many black and ethnic minority, disabled, sexuality and women's activist movements which have influenced policy and academics. Recognising the importance of this work means moving away from presenting minoritised groups as passive victims.

We also cover a range of different perspectives on what causes inequality and discrimination in the workplace. Thus, we provide an overview of economic arguments that derive from Marx and which emphasise the importance of capitalism as an economic system in producing gendered and racialised inequalities and oppression. We also introduce theories which suggest that gendered discrimination is the result of patriarchy and male domination. Subsequently, we show how more cultural theories suggest that gender-, race- and sexuality-based discrimination operate at the symbolic level in the workplace through processes of invisibility and subjectivity. In presenting a range of theories, we are not privileging the need for symbolic equality over economic equality but showing how different theorists separate out these concerns and also bring them together for analytic purposes.

For convenience, we provide an introductory summary at the start of each chapter. We hope you will enjoy the book, and that you find it a useful introduction to gender and diversity in management

.

INTRODUCING GENDER IN MANAGEMENT

Introduction

The focus of Chapter 2 is the concept of 'career' and the notion of equality of opportunity for women. We examine the position of women managers in the labour market and in relation to the corporate boardroom and family business. We look briefly at the women's rights movement, and at the influence of liberal feminism on the equal opportunities agenda. In doing this, we consider the economic history of women's pay and attempt to provide social and economic explanations for women's limited progress in the labour market. To begin with, we examine the history of women's employment. This is because a sense of the historical background to a social issue can be helpful in understanding current events and situations. Thus, we locate the issue of women's employment in its social context, considering the history of women's position in society over the past 150 years, which helps to explain women's constrained progression in the labour market. Secondly, we consider some of the arguments put forward by feminist scholars and activists, including a consideration of the concepts of Marxist feminism, radical feminism and of patriarchy, which present a range of reasons for discrimination against women.

It's All Gone Too Far?

There can be an assumption that women's rights have been achieved and inequality vanquished. If this were the case, there would be no need, at the beginning of the twenty-first century, for feminism, or for any feminist social activism like the women's liberation movement. Admittedly, women's entry to most professions is easier now than it was thirty years ago. Girls are doing well at school and, in the UK, more women than men are going to university. If we look below the surface, however, we observe that all is not as straightforward, or as 'equal', as it may seem. Today, over thirty years since equal opportunities legislation supposedly outlawed discrimination against women managers and promised equal pay regardless of gender, men continue to earn more, and to progress more easily up the career ladder, than women do.

If you turn on the television news or flick through a newspaper, it will be evident that equal opportunities for women in the labour market is still an important issue. This is the case not only in Britain, but in Europe and in the USA. In the corporate world, women Chief Executive Officers are still very few in number, and the gender pay gap (which means that women receive less remuneration than men for doing an equivalent job) still remains a newsworthy issue. It is not uncommon to hear stories of women who lose their jobs when they become pregnant, or of women who are excluded from career opportunities which are on offer to men. In a spate of sex discrimination claims, women bankers are challenging traditional male-dominated cultures in the world of finance, and government think tanks have acknowledged the continued lack of equality of opportunity for women at all levels in the job market (Women and Work Commission 2006).

Thus, there are still a range of problems such as discrimination and inequality in relation to gender. For example, the gender pay gap remains high: on average at just under 20 per cent in the UK for full-time women workers and up to 40 per cent for part-timers (EOC 2005a). In the USA the gender pay gap is even higher, at around 28 per cent for full-time female workers (Padavic and Reskin 2002). Figures provided by the women's labour bureau in the USA demonstrate that qualifications do not necessarily reduce the gender pay gap. In 2003, in America, men with a bachelor's degree or higher qualification earned a median weekly wage of $1,131. Women qualified to bachelor's level or higher earned a median weekly wage of $832 – so, as a percentage, highly qualified women are earning 26.4 per cent less than men (US Department of Labor 2005: 33–4). The gender pay gap affects black and minority ethnic women even more severely than it does white women. For example, in the USA in 1998, as a proportion of men's wages, white women earned 73 per cent, African-American women

63 per cent and Hispanic-American women only 53 per cent (Seager 2005).

With regard to executive status, it remains the case that very few women are appointed to corporate 'top jobs' in Europe and America (Vinnicombe and Bank 2003; Singh and Vinnicombe 2004). In major corporate and professional situations, women often find that their upward progress is blocked (or challenged) when it comes to gaining executive status, while equivalent male colleagues appear to move upwards with comparative ease. A report in *The Economist* (2005) notes that, despite the American government's specially appointed Glass Ceiling Commission (established in 1995 to bring down the barriers that prevented women from reaching the top of the corporate ladder), women account for 46.5 per cent of America's workforce but for less than 8 per cent of its top managers. This figure has altered very little since 1995 when the Commission was set up. In the UK, the situation is similar: while 44 per cent of the workforce is female, very few women command positions on corporate boards. In 2001, only 5 per cent of FTSE 100 companies had more than 20 per cent female directors on their boards, with 43 per cent having no female directors at all (Vinnicombe and Bank 2003). And in 2002, only 61 per cent of the top 100 companies included any female directors at all on their boards – a figure which was down from 64 per cent in 1999 (Singh and Vinnicombe 2004). Even where some improvements can be seen in the numbers of women on corporate boards, the number of female executives remains tiny. For example, between 2000 and 2004 the total number of female executive directors of FTSE 100 companies rose from 11 to 17. However, in comparison with the number of men in such posts (400 male executive directors), even the improved figure could be regarded as negligible (*Economist* 2005: 67). As Jill Treanor, writing in *The Guardian* points out, boardrooms in Britain continue to be afflicted by what she terms as 'pale male' syndrome and there is little sign or promise of change:

> Women are failing to smash through the glass ceiling in FTSE boardrooms, despite attempts to promote diversity at the highest corporate level in Britain ... women [are] losing out in new appointments to the boardroom with only 12.5 of new positions filled by women ... and few women are on the brink of promotion to the top. (Treanor 2006: 3)

Thus, although women may be well qualified, and might work in organisations purporting to have policies which offer equality of opportunity, the career ladder for women in large companies is often foreshortened, while the male ladder extends to the top of the career tree. Women are often hived off into specialist or gendered positions, such as human resources – known as the 'velvet ghetto'. This can have knock-on consequences such as less power and resources, shorter career ladders, less status, less value, less pay and fewer benefits. In sum, women are still segregated vertically in terms of the career ladder and horizontally into particular jobs that are seen as less valued.

During the 1960s, the term 'glass ceiling' was coined to describe the organisational processes that create disadvantage and the difficulties that women face in trying to reach the highest echelons of their particular field. The glass ceiling has been described as a barrier which is transparent but impassable, so that women can see the top of the management hierarchy, but may not reach it. For example, it points to the way that women can find it difficult to obtain the mentoring, training and special project experience that is often needed for advancing in organisations. It is important to note (and we shall discuss this in detail in Chapters 3–5) that for black and minority ethnic women, the situation is even worse, as women in these groups are likely to experience unfair treatment not only because of their gender, but also in relation to their ethnic background. In their research on women's professional identities, Bell and Nkomo (2001) acknowledge the existence of the glass ceiling as a barrier to promotion for all women. However, they suggest that black and minority ethnic women are also faced with a 'concrete wall', meaning that wherever they turn their career progression is limited, and they are prevented by organisational practices and processes from even seeing the top of the career ladder, never mind climbing it.

These processes do not simply operate in large corporate or public services organisations. In both large and small firms, women are often absent at board level within family businesses, where sons continue to take precedence over daughters and where women's contribution is frequently marginalised (Mulholland 1996; Hamilton 2006). This lack of women in executive roles within family businesses is more significant than you might at first imagine. This is because the importance of family businesses to the global economy is to some extent masked, due to the tendency of the financial press to focus on large corporate organisations – a pattern which is replicated in management textbooks. The entrepreneurial literature suggests that the contribution of family firms to global business is huge. Family firms of varying shapes and sizes represent between 75 and 95 per cent of firms registered world-wide and family businesses account for up to 65 per cent of GDP (Howorth et al. 2006). Mulholland (1996) demonstrates how, even though they may resist this as they struggle to claim their place in the family boardroom, female kin in wealthy family firms experience discrimination in terms of both pay and career opportunities as explicitly as if they were employed in the corporate sector:

> **female kin ... play a central and necessary role in the formation of units of wealth, [but find] their efforts appropriated by male kin and their progress stymied when they are marginalised and excluded from the management and ownership of private wealth. (Mulholland 1996: 78)**

Likewise, Hamilton has observed that women are often 'invisible' in the formation of family businesses. Hamilton observes how women may play a fundamental part both in the establishment and the running of family businesses, but are often excluded from the social and economic rewards, working without remuneration and/or being denied partnership status. Hamilton (2006: 8) notes that, where women do achieve social and economic recognition in family firms, this is likely to be difficult to attain and daughters may be obliged to spend years 'working [their way up] due to the requirement to "prove" themselves' in a manner which is not imposed upon male family members. Hamilton acknowledges the difficulties, for women, of fighting male colleagues and bosses within the context of their own families because loyalty to their fathers, brothers and other male kin might pressure daughters and their mothers to 'acquiesce to a particular set of power relations which assume that men [will] lead the business and draw upon the labour and support of female kin' (Hamilton 2006: 9). Hamilton (2006: 15) observes how, frequently, the traditional 'construct/discourse of the "heroic" male owner manager and the invisible woman [is drawn upon] to present the business to the outside world as a particularly recognisable form of organisation', since the preservation of this male narrative enhances the position of the family firm (and consequently profit) within the business world.

The situation is similar in the context of careers which have traditionally been associated with academic qualifications and the 'professions'. While it is true that women are more highly educated now than they were in the past, it remains the case that in most professions, it is men, and not women, who hold the senior, and the most prestigious roles (Edwards and Wajcman 2005; Gatrell 2005). This is especially likely to occur in professions which have traditionally been male preserves, such as medicine, academia, banking and the judiciary. Thus, in higher education, the number of women professors remains low, at around 16 per cent (Association of University Teachers 2003) and there are a few women vice-chancellors. And in politics, the number of female MPs remains consistently less then the number of male MPs, with only around 20 per cent of seats in the British House of Commons held by women (EOC 2005a).

How can we start to understand and explain these statistics? Why are there so few women in senior management roles? Why are black women in a worse position? Why are women segregated into different types of work? There are many different theories which attempt to answer these questions and we turn to these in the sections and chapters below.

Women's Historical Position in the Labour Market

Contemporary discourses [about equal employment opportunities for women] do not sweep away the old world order. They come laden with its resonances. (Hughes 2002: 60)

As the quote above implies, one way to account for these different types of inequality is through examining the history of women's work and education. Historically, women have been associated with homemaking and men with employment. This has been the case not only in middle-class, but also in working-class households, where 'the gradual exclusion of children from the workplace [post-industrial revolution] meant constraints on the labour time and resources of the household, with women carrying the major child-care burden' (Morris 1990: 7). In legal terms, the social position of women was officially inferior to that of men until the last quarter of the twentieth century. The recent history of women's employment provides part of the explanation for why women managers still receive lower levels of pay and opportunity than men – despite legislation which is supposed to prevent discrimination. As Eagly and Karau (2002) and Desmarais and Alksnis (2005) have argued, historical precedents are hard to shift because the habits of the past reproduce the social behaviour of the future. Thus, organisations continue to base their expectations about gender, roles and behaviour on what used to happen in the past:

> organizations and the people within them continue to hold the implicit assumption that the ideal worker is a white man who is employed full time. ... The idea persists that women should be responsible for [the home]. ... We believe that all working woman are violating the normative assumptions of the role of women to some degree. (Desmarais and Alksnis 2005: 459)

Until the late nineteenth century, married women were not permitted to own property, and any money that they inherited, or earned, automatically belonged to their husbands or fathers. From Victorian times to the present date, women were automatically allocated the task of producing and raising the next generation of children, as well as cooking, laundering and cleaning. If they were working class, women were expected to provide supplementary income for the household (but were paid significantly less than men) and were regarded as reserve labour in times of economic growth (Grint 2005). However, middle-class women were not expected to 'go out' to work other than in exceptional conditions, for example when men were away from home fighting wars. In times of war, women of all social classes were encouraged to substitute for men employed in lower-ranking positions (though even during war-time, senior posts were reserved for men). However, women were expected to withdraw gracefully from the labour market when soldiers returned, allowing homecoming men to reclaim available jobs (Summerfield 1998).

We have already acknowledged that, from the mid-1970s onwards (following the enactment of equal rights legislation in the UK and the USA), employed women have had the legal right to expect the same treatment as their male equivalents. However, it is worth pointing out that, until this date in both Britain and America, it was perfectly legal and above board to discriminate against women. Employers could dismiss women, or deny them promotion on grounds of their gender, especially if they were pregnant. Furthermore, employers could (and did) pay women less money than men, even if the women were doing jobs with an equivalent level of responsibility.

Such unequal employment conditions meant that most women were unlikely to be able to afford to run their own homes. Before the Second World War, therefore, women often went into service, or worked in factories for lower pay than men, and many working-class women would have married for economic reasons. Middle- and upper-class women were not expected to 'go out' to work, but to marry and become mothers. Rowbotham (1997: 26), quoting Cicely Hamilton's 1912 advice on 'Marriage as a Trade', observes how '[d]omestic toil was a culture which meant that [poorer] women "learned to look upon [themselves] … as creature[s] from whom much must be demanded and to whom little must be given"'. Those who lived in households where domestic help could be afforded had fewer domestic responsibilities, but precious little else with which to occupy themselves. Rowbotham (1997: 26) recounts how, when the young upper-class Lady Violet Bonham-Carter asked her governess about her future role in life, the governess's answer was clear. 'Until you are eighteen', Violet was told, 'you will do lessons.' 'And Afterwards?' Violet then asked. 'And afterwards,' replied the governess, 'you will do nothing.'

Men at Work, Women at Home

One of the dominant rationales for women's position in the labour market that comes from this kind of historical account is that of socialisation, as introduced in the gender definition in the intro- duction of this book. This is the idea that women are socialised in different ways from men when they are growing up within the home, at school and in wider society. It fits in with the first model of gender discussed in Chapter 1. A historical example of this kind of socialisation, which still has enduring impact, is the so-called image of 'ideal' womanhood which was promulgated from the 1950s through to the early 1970s by the American sociologist Talcott Parsons (Parsons and Bales 1956).

Parsons' work was influential in both Britain and the USA at this time because it offered policy makers a convenient picture of fam- ily life in which heterosexual men and women would marry, have children and share the division of labour in the traditional gendered fashion. The workplace was seen to require characteristics of logic and objectivity, and Parsons and Bales (1956) attributed to men 'Instrumental' traits, meaning that they were ascribed 'rational' psychological attributes and were thus seen to be more suited to the workplace than were women. Husbands were thus employed and fulfilled a public role by going 'out' to work, while wives were allocated the task of fulfilling private, domestic requirements. Parsons and Bales (1956: 163) identified women as inherently 'expressive' or emotional, meaning that they were regarded as unsuited to management roles within the workplace, but were seen to be eminently suitable for the 'integrative-supportive role' within the heterosexual domestic setting (Parsons and Bales 1956: 314). At odds with their argument that women were genetically predisposed to possess 'expressive' qualities, Parsons and Bales underlined social expectations that women should learn and 'develop the skills in human relations which are central to making the home harmonious' (Parsons and Bales 1956: 163). This suggested that expressive skills were not, in fact, innate, but must be acquired through socialisation. Women's role was, therefore, that of housewife, and housewives were expected to clean, shop and bear children (Parsons and Bales 1956). The 'correct' way of performing the role of 'ideal woman' was thus socially defined, and this did not include going out to work or exhibiting work-oriented, ambitious behaviour, as these characteristics were associated only with men (Rich 1977). The idea of 'woman and home' was perpetuated throughout the 1950s, 1960s and 1970s. In popular culture, women were depicted in the maternal domestic role, cooking, cleaning and caring for children, while fathers went out to work (Kerr 2005, originally published 1968).

Parsons and Bales (1956: 14–15) stated:

> The role of housewife is still the ... predominant one for the married woman with small children. ... [T]he adult feminine role is anchored ... in the internal affairs of the family as wife, mother and manager in the household, while the role of the adult male is ... anchored in the occupational world, in his job.

Parsons' idealised picture of family life did not, of course, correspond with the diversity of family practices in 1950s and 1960s Britain or America. Parsons and Bales universalised the concept of 'the family', members of which were, by implication, white, well educated, heterosexual, able-bodied and middle-class. Parsons has been criticised for this failing because, as Giddens (1984: 257) argues: 'Parsons's concentration on normative consensus as the foundation of the integration of societies leads him seriously to underestimate the significance of contestation of norms'. Most importantly in this respect, as Bernardes points out, many 'families' in America were very different from the stereotypical images that Parsons described. Bernardes (1997: 5) observes how:

> In a society with widespread poverty, a large range of ethnic minorities and a large working class, Parsons' claim that: 'It is of course a commonplace that the American family is predominantly and in a sense increasingly an urban middle-class family ... that has emerged a remarkably uniform, basic type of family ... the nuclear family' [seems extraordinary].

Nevertheless, this 'ideal' of the traditional heterosexual family fitted in perfectly with post-war British and American employment policy, which until the mid-1960s was committed to the model of full male employment which came to be a 'taken-for-granted aspect of social and economic life' (Morris 1990: 10). The significance of Parson's work in relation to the social roles of men and women cannot, therefore, be underestimated. While it was unlikely that Parsons wrote with the strategic desire of shaping social behaviours and policy, his work was, nevertheless, highly influential with regard to social practice. It has been suggested by Horna and Lupri (1987) that, whether Parsons intended this or not, his research was responsible for normalising heterosexual roles in which women did housework at home and men were employed. Horna and Lupri (1987: 54) stated: 'Parsons ... has lent credence to role complementarity in the family in assuming that sex-role segregation is necessary for family stability ... husband and wives perform different tasks (functions) that combine to meet all family "needs"'.

Deeply ingrained and historical practices and ideas about the role of women were reflected in the body of scholarly texts about 'work' that were produced during the 1950s, 1960s, 1970s and early 1980s, which focused predominantly on men's paid labour and either ignored women employees altogether, or studied women in relation only to 'normative' male experiences and traits, especially in relation to management (Brewis and Linstead 2004).

This was partly because most women were employed only at the lowliest levels in organisations, meaning that 'classic' texts on managing and decision making never mentioned gender, assuming that 'management' meant 'male', and partly because the male 'norm' of 'rational' decision making and behaviour was regarded as the one best way of managing.

Thus, in historical and legislative practice, in the context of both the Parsonian model of womanhood and scholarly work on management, it can be seen that women were rarely associated with management unless this related to management within the domestic setting. The notion of social exchange, whereby women offered domestic and reproductive labour in exchange for financial support from men, left women in the position where they were utterly dependent upon husbands, and reliant upon men for social status outside marriage. As Morris (1990: 82) points out, the problem with the idea of the exchange of labour between women and men 'causes differential power within marriage [and this] accrues to the male spouse who has the provider role ... the domestic female worker [is] exploited and oppressed'. The advantages, for men, of retaining a situation where they are free from the responsibilities associated with 'low-status, monotonous' housework which 'brings no financial remuneration, is performed to no externally established standards and recei[ves] no recognition' are obvious (Morris 1990: 81).

Thus, even in the twenty-first century, the notion of the female breadwinner contradicts deeply ingrained ideas about the social role of women and provokes challenges from those who might wish to see women more easily confined to the home. The association of women with domestic labour continues to be perpetuated by writers like Tooley (2002), who argues that women are more suited to the domestic environment than they are to paid work, and suggests that women's growing entry into the labour market has served only to cause them unhappiness, a situation which could be reversed if women were to eschew careers in favour of housework: 'there are gender differences in the way men and women respond to domesticity. Many women ... feel [unhappiness] in being moved away from a sphere that could be the source of their fulfilment [the home] to a sphere which is clearly not [employment]' (Tooley 2002: 120).

There are also other important historical workplace gendered inequalities. Summerfield (1998) observes that even during the war years and just after, some professions, such as teaching and the civil service, still had a 'marriage bar', obliging women to leave their employment on marriage. Until the 1970s, it was officially the case that employed women could be dismissed if they became pregnant, and there was no obligation on the part of employers to keep women's jobs open once they had gone on maternity leave. Furthermore, women's part in political processes was almost invisible until after the First World War. Less than 100 years ago, women were denied the right to vote, and even in supposedly 'democratic' countries like Britain and America, only men had the opportunity to elect the (male) politicians whose job it was to run the country. Even when legislation allowing women the vote was enacted in Britain, this applied only to women over 30 years of age and women under 30 were, finally, 'allowed to vote [only] after the passing of the Equal Franchise Act in 1928' (Rowbotham 1997: 121).

In the UK, until the 1970s, university education was open only to the privileged few – and most of the privileged few were men. In the nineteenth century, scholarship was seen to be detrimental to the reproductive function of middle-class women (Showalter and Showalter 1972), and in 1970 Greer noted that:

> **Three times as many girls as boys leave school at fifteen; only one third of A-level students are girls and only a quarter of university students. Three quarters of eighteen year old girls in our society receive no training or higher education at all. (Greer 2006: 132)**

In England, although Cambridge University admitted women to Girton College in 1869, women were not officially 'members' of the university. Thus, while women were allowed to *study* for a degree, only men received the award, and gained the letters after their name. Even when women were allowed to graduate (which in the case of Cambridge students was not until after the Second World War), the numbers of women at university remained limited to around 20 per cent. It was not until the late 1960s and early 1970s that the numbers of women attending university began, gradually, to increase, until we reach the situation today where, in Britain, just over 50 per cent of graduates are female (Dyhouse 2006).

This brief historical overview provides some potential explanations for contemporary workplace discrimination and inequalities but there are other theories and debates to which we turn now, starting with liberal feminism, the concept of patriarchy and radical feminism.

Liberal Feminism and the Origins of 'Equal Opportunities' for Women

Women have always found ways to fight and resist discriminatory practices, individually and collectively, but one very important force in the way that equality, workplace activism and women and work are considered is the women's liberation movement which started in the 1960s and 1970s. As a result of this movement, the notion of equal employment opportunities for women began to impact on public consciousness at the end of the 1960s in both Britain and America (Rowbotham 1997). One significant output of this movement was the idea of expanding the concept of work and workplace to include women's unpaid work at home and in the community as opposed to just paid work in the public sphere. Thus, one important early women's liberation campaign was 'wages for housework': a campaign to show how women 'worked' in the domestic sphere: bringing up children, doing housework, doing emotional labour and undertaking caring work for other dependants and in the wider community. It also emphasised that this 'work' was unpaid but that it enabled men to work in the public sphere, and capitalism to operate, as a result.

There were many different types of feminist thinking within the women's liberation movement. One influential example in 1970s Britain came with Germaine Greer, who raised awareness of women's rights and of the equal opportunities agenda with the publication of her seminal but accessible text *The Female Eunuch* (2006 [1970]). Greer's book called for women to challenge the status quo by exercising their agency and independence, and she argued for women to be offered better opportunities in education and employment. In *The Female Eunuch*, Greer argued that women were undervalued, underpaid and poorly protected by legislation, and she campaigned for employed women to be paid the same as men who were doing equivalent jobs. At the time she wrote it, Greer's book and the improvements in women's circumstances that it proposed were considered to be highly controversial. The notion that women should be afforded equal pay and equal job opportunities caused a storm both politically and among

individual men and women (Greer 2006). Focusing on home relations, another important book was Betty Friedan's *The Feminine
Mystique* (1963), which was widely read and quoted in the USA
and the UK. In Britain and America, the 1960s represented an era
of economic growth, with new career opportunities for men, but
the continued expectation that middle-class women would be eco-
nomically dependent wives whose 'job' was to bear children and
do the housework. Friedan's *The Feminine Mystique* 'gave voice to
many women's previously inchoate longings to move out of the
household and domestic confinement and to participate in an
"equal partnership of the sexes"' (Chancer and Watkins 2006: 31).
These two texts, then, encapsulated certain types of feminist thinking on gender, work and inequality.

Both books can be seen as being influenced by what is known
as a liberal feminist tradition. Liberal feminism is a long-standing
movement which links back to 'first wave' feminist publications
such as Mary Wollstonecraft's *A Vindication of the Rights of Woman*
(2004 [1792]). There are many ways to understand women's inequality
and discrimination, and liberal feminism and its equal opportunities
agenda is a dominant model taken up by some feminist academics
and policy makers. Liberal feminism asserts that women's equality
with men should be achieved through incremental changes in the
education and legal systems. Liberal feminism does not challenge
the categories of 'man' or 'woman' and so does not seek to unset-
tle the gendered binary of organising the world. However, the
liberal feminist argument contends that 'sex', in the biological
sense of being classified as male or female, does not justify sex
discrimination. It argues that men and women are similar, and
women are just as capable of doing any job as a man. Liberal feminism does not reject the idea of society as it is, but seeks some
limited reform of capitalist systems as they currently exist.

The liberal approach to feminism has been criticised from the
1970s onwards because it failed to distinguish between different
groups of 'women' (implying that all women's needs are the
same), and in doing so was seen to privilege white middle-class
women who already had better opportunities than other groups.
Influential US black critical race academic bell hooks, for example,
(1986: 136) points out that if 'poor women had set the agenda for
the feminist movement … class struggle would [have been] a central feminist issue'. Carole Truman, observing contemporary ideas
about equality of opportunity, which sprang from liberal feminist

ideals, contends that equal opportunities policies are most beneficial to 'white, middle class women where the only disadvantage
they experience is based on their gender. "Equality of opportunity"
may only serve those women who are already advantaged by the
class structure and may obscure important differences between
women' (Truman 1996: 42).

Liberal feminism is also seen as overly moderate, because of its
assumption that it is possible to achieve change by working within
(as opposed to transforming) contemporary social systems, working gradually to persuade governments and employers of the need
for incremental change. Thus, hooks has stated:

> I think we have to fight the idea that somehow we have to
> refashion feminism so that it appears not to be revolutionary –
> so that it appears not to be about struggle. … I say the minute
> you begin to oppose patriarchy, you're progressive. If our real
> agenda is altering patriarchy and sexist oppression we are
> talking about a left, revolutionary movement. (1993, quoted in
> Beasley 1999: 31)

However, while liberal feminism may not address the concerns of
feminists who seek fundamental political change through addressing questions of difference, a consideration of liberal feminism is
important in this book in the context of understanding gender in
management. This is because, as Beasley (1999: 53) points out:

> … liberal feminism provides a framework for the development
> of 'moderate' feminist politics and practices which can be
> employed … by government agencies. … Given liberal
> feminism's concern with working for attainable social change
> within the existing confines of modern Western society, it is not
> surprising that … most feminists have made use of this
> framework [and] liberal feminism is the most commonly
> borrowed approach in the feminist pantheon.

For this reason, liberal feminist approaches are most attractive to
policy makers and governing bodies who have a vested interest in
retaining the status quo and who might fear the negative impact,
on them, of major structural changes to society. In our view, feminism and the notion of women's participation in public life remains
a threat to those who continue to see high-level management as a

male preserve. Because they do not promote revolution, but seek only change to existing structures, liberal feminist philosophies offer policy makers the appealing combination of both the least intimidating and the apparently simplest means of accommodating women's requirements to participate in society. Thus, liberal feminist ideas have underpinned many of the equal opportunities policies and practices designed to protect and enhance women's rights to the present day.

Some of the views on the limitations of liberal feminism are shared by the authors of this text, and we go on to explore these in more detail in forthcoming chapters. Like Cockburn (1991), however, we acknowledge that liberal feminist campaigners have fought hard to achieve improvements in many spheres where women have, for centuries, been oppressed, including workplace discrimination and the gender pay gap, divorce and the right to child support, education and occupational segregation.

The liberal feminist movement has made a difference to many women's lives in the twenty-first century. For example, it has assisted important agencies such as the Equal Opportunities Commission in the UK and the Women's Labor Bureau in the USA with arguments and evidence required to shape legislation and battle long-standing inequalities which continue to disadvantage women, such as the right of employers to dismiss pregnant women. Significant changes in UK legislation, such as the Equal Pay Act (passed in 1970; in effect from 1975) and the Sex Discrimination Act (1975), mean that women are supposed to be treated on equal terms with men, and should not experience discrimination in relation to pay or conditions on grounds of their gender (Rowbotham 1997). The ideas of liberal feminism also influence ideas on race, sexuality and disability, and diversity, as we shall see in the next chapter.

Feminist Marxism and Capitalist Relations

Another explanatory framework for analysing gender discrimination in the workplace is Marxism. There are many different versions of Marxism but, in essence, Marxism has been an influential way of understanding class relations and class struggles in the workplace. It is based on the view that capitalism as an economic system is reliant on particular ways of organising work relations or so-called 'relations of production'. Its main focus has been on the exploitation of the working class by the middle class. Feminists have critiqued Marxist thinking for its lack of attention to gender (Barrett 1980, cited in Adkins and Lury 1996; Halford and Leonard 2001). In their view, women's unpaid work in the home is central to enabling men to work and capitalism to continue. Thus, they argue that relations of reproduction, that is the domestic work that women undertake, are essential for continuing the relations of production – in the workplace. The family is understood, ideologically and materially, as central to capitalism. In particular, it is argued that women's unpaid domestic labour, and the gendered division of labour with women doing some jobs and men doing other jobs, mainly in the public sphere, is in the interests of capitalism. Paying for domestic work on the open market would not be seen as in the interests of capitalism (Halford and Leonard 2001). As a result, capitalism keeps women in poorly paid, unskilled and short-term jobs, with few rights and little trade union support so that they can be dispensed with as slumps occur – a process known as a reserve army of labour (Halford and Leonard 2001). Largely an economic theory, feminist Marxism views sexual labour in the home as the main factor in women's discrimination and inequality in the workplace. In this view, gender is reproduced through and because of the needs of capitalism (Adkins and Lury 1996).

Patriarchy and Women's Oppression

Having discussed liberal feminism as one way of understanding inequality, we now turn to another way of explaining discrimination in the workplace: patriarchy. While some feminist scholars attribute unequal relations between women and men to class and capitalism, others suggest that 'the source of women's oppression and domination as unpaid labourers', in circumstances where contemporary women still have less opportunity than their male counterparts to attain 'executive' public positions, 'is not capitalism but patriarchy' (Morris 1990: 83). Without denying the importance of class or ethnicity (or claiming that patriarchy is the only explanation for gender subordination), feminist writers such as Walby (1990) have contended that patriarchy nevertheless pervades all aspects of life and education. They argue that 'the concept of "patriarchy" is indispensable for an analysis of gender inequality

(Walby 1990: 1). Although the subject of much debate, the theory of patriarchy seeks to explain why and how women still experience inequality and discrimination. In essence, patriarchy is understood as a system of social structures and practices which are used by men to dominate and oppress women (Walby 1990). In the workplace, the notion of patriarchy explains, in part, how women's economic and personal needs are subordinated to those of men.

For some theorists, patriarchy is so much a part of everyday lives that it operates as a fundamental socialisation system: both men and women are seen as being locked into traditional sex roles from an early age, via education systems. Davies and Banks (1992: 45) argue that, from the age of 4 and earlier, children are 'informed by powerful discourses of gender. It is the power of those discourses to trap children within conventional meanings and modes'. Scraton (1990: 90) asserts that patriarchal values are ingrained in young people via the schools system. She argues that girls and young women are persuaded by physical education, at school, to believe that they are 'weaker, less powerful' than men, and suggests that (especially sports) 'teachers [may] justify their practice of stereotyping and use biology as an explanation even though their own ... experiences [are] at variance with their views' (Scraton 1990: 91). Thus, women become used to being patronised and excluded from social opportunities from childhood (and men become used to excluding them) because their future reproductive status is regarded as a constraint from a very early age: 'gender needs to be theorised as being structured by a dominant hegemonic masculinity which not only forms the basis of male–female relationships but also is conveyed and internalised through institutions' (Scraton 1990: 91). In this view, patriarchal ideologies and relations take hold through home and school socialisation.

Patriarchal theorists suggest that matters do not improve for those women who, once they leave the education system, enter into employment. There are seen to be a range of patriarchal relations in paid work, including the practices which create vertical and horizontal job and occupation segregation. 'Accepted' practices in the workplace continue to discriminate against women while masquerading as apparently non-gendered policies, with women's identity as potential childbearers overriding other issues such as equal opportunities. As Cockburn (2002: 180) has reflected:

Even if the woman ... is celibate or childless, she is seen and represented as one of the maternal sex. Much of the argument surrounding Equal Opportunities at work circles about the question: can women *ever* be equal, given their different relation to reproduction? (original emphasis)

Writers such as Cockburn (2002) and Walby (1990) consider that it is not women's reproductive status which limits their power, but repressive social systems of male domination. In accordance with this view, Sylvia Walby (1990: 67) suggests that: 'Motherhood as an institution under patriarchy does give women a lot of problems, but this is due to patriarchy, not to motherhood itself. There is nothing essentially oppressive about children'. In this view, patriarchy is a systemic system of domination which structures all walks of life, including the workplace.

Radical Feminism

Descriptions of patriarchy are associated with a radical form of feminism. Radical feminists differentiate themselves from histories or theories based on the previous development of 'malestream' thought (such as Marxism), and believe that 'it is gender relations rather than class relations that generate fundamental inequalities in the social world' (Porter 1998: 186). In this view, it is not capitalism but men as a group who dominate women. Radical feminism is a departure from liberal feminism because radical feminists regard the assertion of women's rights through incremental policy changes to be overly accepting of the status quo which places men, and male needs, at the centre of society and social policy. Radical feminists 'give a positive value to womanhood rather than supporting a notion of assimilating women into areas of activity associated with men' (Beasley 1999: 54). Women are understood as having different experiences, interests and ways of being from men. Radical feminism regards 'women's oppression [as] the oldest, most widespread, the most obdurate and the most extreme form of oppression that exists between humans' (Porter 1998: 186) and radical feminists insist that 'the distinguishing character of women's oppression is their oppression as women, not as members of other groups such as their social class' (Beasley 1999: 54). Rather than trying to be the same as men, therefore, radical feminists celebrate

the concepts of womanhood and sisterhood. While it is acknowledged by recent writers that 'women' cannot be treated as a
homogeneous group (Beasley 1999), radical feminists nevertheless
focus on 'women's similarities and the pleasures of forming ...
bonds between women in a world where such bonds are marginalised or dismissed' (Beasley 1999: 54). Thus, special groups of
women, such as lesbians and mothers, are celebrated by radical
feminists on the basis that they have unique characteristics associated with womanhood that men cannot share.

Some of the key early writers on women's domestic and reproductive labour, such as Rich (1977) and Oakley (1981), embraced
the politics of radical feminism, celebrating womanhood and
motherhood, and challenging patriarchy as they sought to pursue
'revolutionary practice ... with an emphasis on small group organisation ... stress[ing] practical political strategies and ... focus[ing]
on *the politics of the "private" sphere*, in particular sexuality, motherhood and bodies' (Beasley 1999: 56–7, original emphasis).

In accordance with some elements of radical feminist beliefs,
we consider society to be inherently patriarchal, with the scales
loaded against women who seek to achieve equal status in almost
any field: 'men as a group dominate women as a group and are
the main beneficiaries of the subordination of women' (Walby
1990: 3). Informed by the work of writers such as Rich (1977),
Oakley (1981) and Firestone (1970), we acknowledge that the
roots of patriarchy are inextricably linked with women's reproductive status, and with the female body. At the same time, however,
we suggest that there are problems associated with radical feminism which, with its all-embracing approach, may privilege the
voices of some women at the expense of other groups, for example
black and minority ethnic, and disabled women. bell hooks, for
example, has argued for a black feminist political agenda since the
beginning of the 1980s (hooks 1981), although at the same time as
emphasising the difference between black and white feminist politics,
hooks remains concerned at the notion that women's differences
make feminist unity impossible because too much fragmentation
may weaken the feminist movement. Other feminist writers see
cohesion between mainstream (usually white) and other groups of
women as problematic, on the basis that the needs of the minority
group will be suppressed. Annecka Marshall, for example, observed
in 1994 how mainstream sociological and feminist approaches to
research on gender 'do not sufficiently examine the experiences of

black women', who are often 'excluded from the creation of socio-logical and feminist thought' (Marshall 1994: 106, 108).

In summary, then, there have been many positive changes for women since Friedan and Greer wrote their famous texts, and there are many more opportunities for women within the labour market than there were in 1970. Probably for the very reason that it advocates incremental progress within traditional social con-texts, liberal feminism has facilitated significant change and remains the favoured approach among policy makers and govern-ing bodies. However, despite improvements in women's position in the labour market, progress remains limited and the 'top' jobs within industry, family business and the professions continue to be filled not by non-mothers, or women with children, but by men. When it comes to very senior public roles in society, women have not achieved equality of opportunity and the 'glass ceiling' and concrete and maternal walls remain firmly in place. These views focus on how gendered practices in organisations are shaped by wider social, economic and cultural processes. In the next chap-ter, while not letting go of this emphasis, we turn to theories on gender which focus on how organisational settings themselves actively create gendered practices which then, in turn, feed into other arenas. Partly due to the slow pace (and the resulting slow progress) of the liberal feminist/equal opportunities agenda, but partly also because liberal feminist approaches fail to differentiate between different groups of women, many feminist scholars are developing ideas which depart from the liberal feminist notion that women can make gradual progress towards equality with men through incremental changes in the educational and legal systems and without changing conventional social norms. In Chapters 3–5 we discuss how scholarship and new ideas have begun to impact on both scholarship and on the policy agenda.

GENDER IN MANAGEMENT: SOCIAL AND CULTURAL PERSPECTIVES

Introduction

In the previous chapter we outlined some dominant historical perspectives on gender in relation to the workplace. In this chapter,
we do not suggest that these ideas are no longer helpful. However,
we now offer some more contemporary thinking on gender and
gendering in the workplace. We start with current ideas on the
domestic sphere. As we suggested in Chapter 2, women's supposed
place in the home has been seen as one way of understanding
inequality and discrimination in the workplace. It is often suggested
that there have been many changes since the 1950s in how
women's work at home affects their work, opportunities and experience of the paid workplace. Our first section presents a range of
theories which indicate that maybe the changes haven't been so
radical as is sometimes imagined. We go on to consider the relationships between employment and family practices. In this context
we also think about the impact on men of social and organisational
expectations about gender, and how men 'should' behave. We
touch on what implications the gendered division of labour may
have for men in organisations, and how this affects both men and
women who are combining caring roles with paid work. We then
turn to cultural analyses of gender, introducing ideas on the body
and masculinity. Finally, we think about how traditional stereotypes
of the gendered body might influence the roles that are available in
professional and/or managerial fields.

Discrimination: Motherhood and Management

Pringle (1998) and others (Williams 1999; Blair-Loy 2003; Gatrell
2005, 2007a, 2007b) have argued that the career progress of

women in management and/or the professions is especially likely to stall if they become mothers. Equal opportunities laws are supposed to protect women against discrimination on the grounds of pregnancy and motherhood. The law states that employers are not allowed to dismiss a woman for being pregnant, nor should she be disadvantaged in terms of pay or promotion. In practice, however, the protection offered to women in the workplace is limited. Figures produced by the Equal Opportunities Commission in the UK demonstrate that every year 30,000 British women face discrimination during, and immediately following, pregnancy, often resulting in dismissal (EOC 2005a).

Mothers in management roles appear extremely vulnerable to unfair treatment during pregnancy, with one-third experiencing discrimination, as opposed to one-fifth of pregnant women overall (EOC 2005a). Mothers often experience the worst problems when they return to work after maternity leave, especially if they seek to work part-time in a managerial or professional context (EOC 2005a, 2005b; BBC News 2005). Dex et al. (1998) observe how many organisations espouse generous work–family policies, which claim to support the *principle* of part-time working. However, Blair-Loy (2003), Williams (1999), Williams and Cohen Cooper (2005) and Gatrell (2005, 2007a) observe that organisational equal opportunities policies often lack detail. They may thus, for example, acknowledge the right of workers to request part-time or flexible working, but may refuse to implement this in practice. They may also neglect to articulate what their approach will be to workers who access the right to work part-time (for example, when children are very young) but who subsequently seek to return to a full-time post. Furthermore, the establishment of workable criteria for the promotion of part-time staff is rare and, as we suggest below, women who work part-time are likely to find their career prospects looking somewhat gloomy. In practice, women who work part-time may well find that career opportunities are limited in management and professional and non-managerial roles.

For example, Pringle (1998) has explored issues of gender and inequality within the medical profession. She argues that although 'lip-service' is paid to supporting women doctors (Pringle 1998: 9), this is not reflected in practice. This is because women are continually undermined by what she describes as the 'male medical establishment', which remains determined to adhere to traditional ways of recruitment, selection and practising – all of which disadvantage women, especially those who have children. Pringle, who examines the medical establishment in both Britain and Australia, observes explicit 'medical resistance to women doctors' (Pringle 1998: 10). Making observations about medicine which are similar to the points made by Hamilton (2006) about family businesses, Pringle suggests that conventional medical hierarchies and structures force women to 'work harder and longer than men' if they are to achieve recognition and career status as doctors – especially if they seek to become hospital consultants.

Pringle suggests that the medical profession is particularly disapproving of women who combine motherhood with medicine. Women who have babies are expected to 'take off extraordinarily little time for the birth of their children' (Pringle 1998: 12). Pringle observes that women doctors who seek to work flexibly are particularly unpopular (often mothers, but presumably also those with other caring responsibilities). This is due not only to the specific changes in working practices that would be needed to accommodate part-time working for hospital doctors, but because such requests symbolise the encroachment of women into a profession previously regarded as a high-status, male preserve: 'women's demands for a restructuring of medical time strike at the heart of the medical sublime' (Pringle 1998: 10). Thus, the number of women admitted into esteemed medical specialties such as obstetrics and neurology remains very small. And while staffing shortages and the lack of evidence-based arguments have obliged the male medical establishment to accept the notion of women GPs, some influential male doctors remain opposed to the idea of women as family doctors because of the possibility that they may at some point become mothers, and may then wish to work flexibly. In 2002, for example, a member of the GP Committee of the British Medical Association is reported as having stated that medical school entry should be made more difficult for women than for men. The committee member argued:

> Medical Schools should discriminate against women to help tackle the shortage of GPs because women take more career breaks than men and work part-time more often. ... Positive discrimination towards men training as doctors would help solve the staffing crisis. This is not about misogyny, it's about the future of the medical workforce. (quoted in Gatrell 2005: 60).

In this quote, and through the practices which support it, women are seen to be the problem, rather than society's approach to childcare or the medical profession's approach to difference.

Part-time Work

> Many feminists have noted how the whole notion of 'career'
> is gendered and centred on male norms of continuous
> employment, full-time work and progression through
> increasing levels of job responsibility. (Truman 1996: 40)

This quote highlights the way that 'career' and 'part-time' are often
imagined as a contradiction in terms. Given that the group most
likely to be working part-time are women with young children, ideas
of part-time professional and managerial work and discrimination
are closely entangled with the issue of motherhood. Edwards and
Wajcman (2005) suggest that all women may experience constraints
on their career progress, regardless of whether or not they have
children. However, Davidson and Cooper (1992) and Desmarais and
Alksnis (2005) argue that mothers in management and the professions experience even worse levels of discrimination than career
women with no children. It has been further argued (Williams 1999;
Blair-Loy 2003; Gatrell and Cooper 2007) that unfavourable treatment
towards senior career mothers will be exacerbated if they work
part-time, as this inevitably means that mothers deviate from the
long-hours cultures which are increasingly the 'norm' within the
management context. Thus, mothers working less than full-time are
disadvantaged in labour markets and the combination of motherhood and part-time working is often regarded by employers as being
incommensurate with senior-level employment (as demonstrated in
the work of Lewis (2006), Williams (1999) and Blair-Loy (2003)).

Various explanations are offered as to why this should be the
case. These include the suggestion that employers' refusal to promote women working part-time is due both to inaccurate views
regarding mothers' lack of commitment to their paid work and the
employers' fears that women working part-time will be unreliable
and unambitious.

Women's Work Orientation

The argument that women working part-time are unambitious and
uncommitted to their paid work is associated principally with the
work of Catherine Hakim. Hakim's research is significant because
it has formed the basis of advice to influential UK agencies, such
as the Institute of Directors (Hakim 1996a; Malthouse 1997), which
seek to influence government policy on employers' behalf.

At the heart of Hakim's argument is her belief that women are oriented towards home and family, and men towards paid employment. Reproducing an individual preference model of gender, as discussed in the introduction, Hakim suggests that women have a lower work-orientation than men do, and that part-time women employees (especially those with children) are less committed to their paid work than full-timers. Hakim considers this argument to potentially apply to the work orientation of women of all classes and occupations, and in the case of those in managerial and professional roles she suggests that careers and associated higher education are attractive because these offer access to 'elite marriage markets' and provide 'an insurance policy' in the event of divorce (Hakim 2000: 37). Statistical claims that female employment is rising are fairly well founded, but in 1995, Hakim challenged the basis for this view (Hakim 1995). Hakim's argument was challenged by Ginn et al. (1996), who suggested that Hakim's hypothesis was flawed because it declined to acknowledge the number of women in part-time posts and it failed to observe the increase in women's commitment to paid work. Hakim responded by asserting that:

> **The unpalatable truth is that a substantial proportion of women still accept the sexual division of labour which sees homemaking as women's principal activity and income earning as men's principal activity in life. The acceptance of differentiated sex roles underlines fundamental differences between the work orientations, labour market behaviours and life goals of men and women. (Hakim 1996b: 179)**

More recently, Hakim (2000) has suggested that most women's low commitment to paid work can be explained through preference theory. Fundamental to the idea of preference theory is the notion that women have free choice about whether or not to 'go out' to work, this choice being unencumbered by social and economic circumstances (a hypothesis which might be contested by scholars writing about patriarchy, such as Walby (1990)).

Hakim concludes that only 20 per cent of women are work-oriented, with 20 per cent home-oriented and the remainder treating employment as a 'job' rather than a 'career'. Hakim focuses particularly on mothers and claims that women with children lose interest in paid work following childbirth. Hakim's claims do not go uncontested. For example, McRae (2003: 592) has challenged Hakim's arguments around women, employment and notions of 'choice', and Williams (1999), Gatrell (2005), Blair-Loy (2003) and Singh and Vinnicombe (2004) all provide evidence which is contrary to Hakim's thesis. These writers argue, from a range of perspectives, that women managers who are also mothers may be highly ambitious, regardless of whether or not they work part-time for a period. Nevertheless, the fear that mothers may be uncommitted to their paid work runs very deep and is not confined to Hakim's research, but is widely held among employers and professional bodies. We have already acknowledged Pringle's observation that the medical profession continues to resist the notion of the senior women doctors, an issue which, Pringle suggests, 'now centres on the issue of part-time work' (Pringle 1998: 10). This attitude is mirrored in other fields, such as academia and law, where mothers who work part-time may be regarded as unambitious, 'marginal', 'unavailable' and 'weak women who will be forever grateful' for being permitted to work less than full-time (Birnie et al. 2005: 255).

Interlinked with ideas about mothers' work orientation (or lack thereof) there is often an expectation on the part of employers that mothers in professional and managerial roles should regard the option of working part-time as a privilege, for which they must pay a price. In return for the 'privilege' of working part-time (even if this is only for a limited period) women managers are often expected to 'sacrifice upward mobility' in the long term (Blair-Loy 2003: 92). Blair-Loy describes how, as a consequence of this approach, mothers working part-time are often placed on the 'mommy track', an option which is 'lacking in career advancement possibilities' but which demands hard work, a proven track record of experience in the field and excellent qualifications.

Women Without Children

> The impact of motherhood shadows every woman, narrowing her options. [Women] without children may [nevertheless] be harmed: the mere fact that they are of childbearing age may compromise their career prospects. (Williams 1999: 70)

What of women who do not have children? Can we assume that, for this group, the career path will be smooth? Will their non-mother status entitle them to the same treatment as men in equivalent managerial and professional roles? Unfortunately, both the statistics on women's work, which we described above, and qualitative studies on childless women and employment suggest that women's childless status does not necessarily enhance their career prospects. This is because organisations and employers have been shown to discriminate against women on the grounds of the *possibility* that women could, at some point, have a child. In a confidential survey undertaken by the Institute of Directors, it was shown that 45 per cent of the Institute's membership would be reluctant to employ any woman aged between 16 and 49 years in case she might become pregnant (Malthouse 1997). It is recognised by Cockburn (2002), Wajcman (1998), Williams (1999) and Tyler (2000) that women's reproductive status and their *potential* for maternity (regardless of whether or not they ever have children) is sufficient to disadvantage them. Wajcman (1998: 143) has argued: 'In terms of occupational advancement … women's sacrifice of a family life is in vain. They face the same prejudices as other women even though they have refused the mantle of mother and wife.'

Unfairly, at the same time as experiencing discrimination because they may one day have children, women who counter such assumptions by making public declarations about their non-motherhood are unlikely to be welcomed by organisations as leaders of the future. Instead, as Hughes (2002: 61) points out, they will probably be regarded as 'selfish' and incapable of performing their femininity correctly: 'Selfish non-mother discourses speak to an absence of [feminine] selflessness in the character of [non-mothers]. These women are portrayed as caring more for their own comforts than for those of others.'

Furthermore, non-motherhood does not necessarily entitle women to undertake the career-advancing tasks which are most commonly reserved for men. Ramsay and Letherby (2006), who identify non-mothers as a social group within organisations, observe how professional women who do not have children may still be regarded, by line managers, in a 'motherly' light. Non-mothers carry the weight of expectations that they will undertake pastoral and day-to-day administrative tasks in the workplace, leaving male colleagues free to lead new and more challenging projects. In career terms, pastoral and everyday responsibilities are not regarded in the same prestigious light as are new and challenging projects. Thus, women who are not mothers will nevertheless find that career progression is limited.

In addition, women managers who adopt the behaviours associated with successful 'masculine' management may be accused of failing to perform their 'feminine' role 'properly', because ambition and success are regarded as appropriate characteristics for men, but not for women, to possess (Nelson and Quick 1985; Davidson and Cooper 1992; Desmarais and Alksnis 2005). Women leaders (both those with and those without children) are often accused of, and censured for, adopting behaviours associated with masculinity. This is an argument which women cannot 'win' because their reproductive status will usually be cited as justification for condemning women who adopt a 'masculine' management style, in the sense identified by Kerfoot (2000). Thus, childless women without male partners who work long hours and foreground careers over personal life may be labelled as being 'not quite normal' (Davidson and Cooper 1992: 134). Conversely, female managers who are also mothers, and who attempt to keep pace with the long-hours cultures and requirements to appear unemotional and 'in control' at work are often accused of selfish behaviour and of failing their children, and thereby society (Gatrell 2005).

It has already been observed that employers fight shy of hiring women due to their physical capacity for motherhood, which is considered 'taboo' in the workplace (Martin 1992) and which is linked to both ideas of patriarchy and women's role in social history as homemakers. Focusing on motherhood, feminist writers in the 1970s (Rich 1977; Oakley 1981) have drawn extensively on the idea of the female body, which they regarded as a 'site of struggle' (Nast and Pile 1998: 2). Some early radical feminist writers, such as Firestone (1970) and Valeska (1975), have argued that women should not be obligated to bear or raise children but should be enabled by society to pursue their careers as a priority. Firestone (1970: 270), long before the advent of new reproductive technologies, argued for 'the freeing of women from the tyranny of their biology by any means available, and the diffusion of the childbearing and child-rearing role to society as a whole'. Other writers, such as Rich (1977) and Oakley (1981, 1984), while they embraced feminist politics and resisted patriarchal traditions nevertheless celebrated maternity as a valuable characteristic of womanhood, which men could not share. These writers believed that women who wished to bear children should have the right to experience motherhood without having to sacrifice careers. In sum, there are several factors which may explain why women still take on most of the childcare responsibilities, including historical factors, discourses on good mothering, structures of childcare, symbolism of bodies, essentialist assumptions about women's nurturance and maternalism, among others.

Many of the theories covered so far assume that gender is something which men and women possess, which then affects them in the workplace. There is a contrasting view that aspects of organisations produce and reproduce gender. It is to these theories that we now turn.

Gender is What We Do and Think in Organisations

In this view of gender in the workplace, taken from the work of Acker (1990) and Gherardi (1995), actions, cultures, practices, ways of organising and events can be seen as gendered and 'engendering' (Bruni and Gherardi 2002: 21). Formal organisations produce and reproduce gendered structures and processes: as Acker (1992: 249) puts it, 'many apparently gender-neutral processes are sites of gender production'. Gendered processes are concrete formal and informal activities and events in the workplace; what people say and do, and how they think (Acker 1992). This means that many formal and informal practices are partially structured on the basis of gender constructions – ideas about men, women, femininity, masculinity, race, sexuality, class and able-bodiedness. They can be overt or covert, and may not be recognised as having anything to do with gender. They create particular types of relations between men and women, ideas about proper roles for men and women and incorporate notions about gender in everyday actions, rules and events. In addition, they engender (that is reproduce certain ways of 'doing' one's gender properly) through participation in the workplace (Acker 1992). This model moves away from individualistic or interactional views of gender to focus on the institutional and practice-based idea of gendering. Rather than emphasising the socialisation of children in the home or school, gender is seen as something produced through daily workplace practices in a dynamic, concrete and contradictory way, working with and through other social categories such as race, class, sexuality and able-bodiedness. Theorists working with this perspective focus on ongoing processes that produce social categories, rather than understanding race, gender etc. as fixed or essentialist traits or qualities or understanding the work-place as a gender-neutral place in which gendered actors behave (McDowell 1999).

Feminist sociologist Joan Acker is one of the leading theorists in this area. One of her most influential ideas was to show how jobs – imagined to be gender-neutral – are profoundly gendered. Thus, in a highly cited paper (Acker 1990), she suggests that the supposed abstract category of 'a job' or 'a worker' is in fact highly gendered. What she means by this is that the construct of a job, or the 'ideal' worker, in much theory and practice can only be filled by a 'disembodied' worker without any outside obligations (1990: 149). Women can't be seen as disembodied workers because they are imagined as profoundly embodied with obligations outside work in the home or community. In relation to the notion of ideal worker, therefore, women are seen as marginal and 'other'. There is, in her view, already a gender-based division of labour in the home and workplace embedded in the notion of a 'job'. In sum, for Acker, jobs and workers are 'deeply gendered and bodied' (1990: 150). Acker's work points to the gendered nature of the economic domain, often imagined as ungendered (Adkins and Lury 1996).

Other gendered and gendering processes in the workplace have been identified by Acker and others (1990, 1992). These include gender divisions – the way that jobs, pay, hierarchies and power are patterned by gender – and symbols and images – gender images, metaphors, language and symbols which reinforce or justify gender divisions. For example, senior leaders are imagined as being strong, rational, decisive and forceful; strategy is understood through military metaphors and organisations are viewed through masculine imagery of being goal-oriented, aggressive, lean and mean (Acker 1992). Another gendering process for Acker is interaction between individuals, women and men, men and men, and women and women. This fits with the model of gender described in Chapter 1. These interactions take multiple forms but enact power and domination, create alliances and exclusions, and affirm policies and gendered images and sexual relations (Acker 1992). These processes, according to Acker, build on and produce what she calls a gendered substructure of an organisation. This substructure is embedded in workplace rules, spatial and temporal arrangements of work and other practices and relations.

Cultural Processes of Gender in the Workplace

In contrast to feminist theories which focus on economic or social explanations for gendering in the workplace, there is a range of feminist theorists who examine the cultural processes and mechanisms which create practices, languages and values that lead to systems of inequality. In this view, culture is understood as the main determinant of gender. Hence, gender is seen as a cultural and symbolic process (Adkins and Lury 1996). For example, theorists may look at how masculine values and power are reinforced through jokes or harassment in the workplace. Cultural and symbolic resources are seen as central to the construction of jobs and workplace identities. Thus, certain types of imagery or language are seen as a way of enforcing masculine identities and values: for example, the discourse of 'gender neutrality' in organisations. There is also an exploration in this kind of work on the cultural forms of masculinity and femininity: for example, the different types of masculinity and femininity in different organisations and what these are seen to mean. This analysis can also be extended to examine how things and actions can be understood as masculine or feminine (Alvesson and Due Billing 2002). For instance, Sylvia Gherardi (1995) argues that organisational cultures provide discursive and symbolic resources – often conflicting resources – through which gender is produced. Her focus is on men's and women's selves and how they feel and think (their subjectivities) and how these are produced through workplace engendering processes.

Research may also focus on what are known as 'discourses'. These are ways of speaking and writing about people, objects and reality that produce 'truths' about them. These, in turn, create particular ways of thinking, being and acting. Thus, discourses are understood as productive. This means that they create what they claim to describe. In this way, organisational discourses about men and women or masculinity and femininity are seen to create particular ways of thinking about and doing masculinity and femininity while marginalising other forms of gender. Identities are seen to be achieved through different discourses – both explicit discourses on gender and other, more workplace-oriented discourses which implicitly produce ideas about gender. An example of this type of research is Rosemary Pringle's (1989) work on the discourses of secretary–boss relationships in which she examined the symbolism (the sexual and family imagery drawn upon by female secretaries and their male bosses) and the ways in which cultural meanings structured these relationships and positioned men and women in specific roles. In particular, she emphasises how these meanings and discourse positions reproduced specific types of gendered power and behaviours, through which male bosses control female secretaries. Power, in this view, is seen as the effect of gendered discourses.

In the following sections, we continue to profile cultural analyses of gender in the organisation by providing an overview of theorists who focus on the body and others who examine masculinity as a workplace identity. These move beyond simply looking at cultural, symbolic or discursive processes to include other, more material perspectives too. This is because, for some feminists, we need to recognise that gender does not emerge from one source (that is, the cultural) and, in addition, we need to emphasise how the cultural is not universally available to all as a resource for making identities in the workplace (Adkins and Lury 1996).

Women's Bodies 'Out of Place'

Since 2000, there has been a renewed surge of interest in the relationships between women's bodies and women's public role in society (for example, Moi 2005; Swan 2005; Young 2005; Puwar 2004; Longhurst 2001). Nirmal Puwar (2004), in her study of the experiences of British female MPs, scrutinises what happens when white and black women enter workplace spaces which have conventionally been the preserve of white, male professionals. Puwar refers to white and black women who occupy traditionally male and public arenas as 'space invaders', and observes that verbal attacks on women may be mediated through their bodies (with women MPs especially vulnerable to abuse if they discuss issues specifically related to sexual politics). Puwar observes how white men have comfortably inhabited positions of leadership for centuries. Men have thus become the 'somatic norm' in organisational roles involving management and decision making. This means that when 'women and racialised minorities' enter the workplace in a role which could be equated with leadership, they are likely to be treated as 'outsiders' because their womanhood makes them very visible or 'marked' (Puwar 2004: 8). In the context of the 'ideal' employed body, Puwar (2004: 59) observes that 'the bodies of women are a liability' because in order to be accepted in the workplace as managers and decision makers 'the ideal representatives of humanity are those who are not marked by their body, and whose bodies are "invisible"'.

Puwar (2004) and Longhurst (2001) have both observed how women in management roles find themselves under continual pressure to blend in with male bodily 'norms', while at the same time being expected to perform their femininity to an appropriate standard. Longhurst (2001: 102–3) explains how senior women are expected to downplay their sexuality in the office, due to the need to 'dress in a way that enhances [their] … professional image' but observes how, concurrently,

> **If professional women completely emulate men, with no touches of the feminine, such as … a skirt instead of trousers, small heels instead of flat shoes, they are often constructed as too 'hard', as 'butch', or as second rate men. They become women cross-dressed as men and as such are subject to ridicule.**

Conversely, however, writers such as Martin (1992), Young (2005), Tyler (2000) and Gatrell (2007a, 2007b) suggest that even those women who wish to manage their female bodies so as to 'fit into' the traditionally male space of management and the professions will find this hard, especially in cases where their reproductive functions become difficult to hide, such as when they are pregnant or breast-feeding. As Höpfl and Hornby Atkinson observe, mothers with small children, or pregnant women, may find it almost impossible obscure their 'biology, [which] relegates women to the status of inferior men' (Höpfl and Hornby Atkinson 2000: 135).

Furthermore, women's bodies at work are often, still, highly sexualised, especially if they are fulfilling junior roles such as receptionist, secretary or waitress. In office situations, women are expected to wear clothing which emphasises their femininity, while simultaneously conforming to male practices (Longhurst 2001; Puwar 2004). In the leisure industry, (especially young) female bodies may be seen as objects of desire and women may be required to accept male behaviours verging on sexual harassment as 'part of the job' (Adkins 1995).

Men, Masculinity and Organisations

At the end of this discussion on women in management (and before we move on to consider issues of diversity) we take some time to explore the situation of male managers and professionals within organisations. We have already established that, in terms of status and remuneration, senior men appear to be doing well in comparison with senior women. Men are often paid more than women in equivalent roles and men are more likely than women to be mentored, and to be offered career opportunities, especially if they are white, healthy and able-bodied. Some writers argue, however, that while being male offers managers higher income and better prospects, the 'masculine norms' which underpin organisational behaviour – in particular, long-hours cultures and the requirement to conform to what Longhurst (2001: 103) describes as 'the gendered politics of dress' – may be constraining for some men.

For some men who seek senior management and/or professional roles, the pressures of conforming to the Parsonian image of the heterosexual, married or co-habiting economic provider can prove limiting and restrictive. As we shall discuss in Chapters 4 and 5, for men with caring responsibilities, for gay men or black men, or for men who wish to pursue other interests alongside employment, the assumption that male managers are also, inevitably, white, be-suited, heterosexual breadwinners may cause real problems of inequality and disadvantage. In the last ten years, there has been a growth in research on men and masculinities. Connell (1995), Haywood and Mac an Ghaill (2003) and Whitehead (2005) all challenge the notion that there is only one way of understanding masculinity. The work of these scholars explores the role and the situation of men in society from a range of perspectives, and this leads to the conclusion that the traditional masculine role, as described by Parsons, is embodied, idealised and may be problematic for many men, particularly if they feel obliged to try to 'meet [contemporary] hegemonic standards' (Connell 1995: 54).

Ideas on masculinity have recently been taken into discussions on management and organisational theory. For example, Edwards and Wajcman (2005: 80) have observed that 'management' has for many years 'been equated with masculinity'. Edwards and Wajcman argue that the concept of masculinity in managerial terms centres not only on the cultivation of a masculine appearance, but also around particular traits associated with the masculine manager: being rational, logical, objective and 'in control'. Similarly, Kerfoot and Knights (1993, 1996; see also Swan 2005) have suggested that 'masculinity' is not a genetic characteristic common only to men. Rather, 'masculinity' in management is more akin to a performance, with 'masculine' men constantly under pressure to maintain the 'masculine' identities associated with the management role. This interpretation accords with Connell's (1995: 54) description of the embodiment of masculinity in sport as a metaphor for men's social performance of masculinity, which reproduces patterns of male hegemony. Connell observes how men's

> **whole pattern of body development and use [and] ... the institutional organization of sport embeds definite social relations: competition and hierarchy among men, exclusion or domination of women. These social relations of gender are both realized and symbolized in bodily performance. ... At the same time, bodily performances are called into existence by these structures and the constitution of masculinity through bodily performance means that gender is vulnerable when the performance cannot be sustained, for instance as a result of physical disability.**

We shall consider the situation of gay men in more detail in Chapter 5. However, at this stage it is worth noting Connell's (1995) observation that contemporary gay men experience discrimination in the job market and may be vilified in the media. Connell (1995: 40) argues that 'the point of these practices is not just to abuse individuals. It is to draw social boundaries, defining "real" masculinity by its distance from [gay masculinity]'. Men are expected to give the impression of being 'in control' of emotions, health and bodily functions. 'Masculinity' is often associated with long hours in the workplace and with the requirement to present an image of a man who is prepared to sacrifice family and personal time for the needs of the employer. Collinson and Collinson (2004) describe this phenomenon as 'presenteeism'. Brewis and Linstead (2004) have observed a trend for managers to be seen to be developing 'emotional awareness', but note that this is only in the context of an overall masculine performance, and *only* in the context of paid work. 'Emotional awareness' does not mean spending more time with friends, family and partners. This might seem surprising in the context of recent debates concerning work–life balance and the need for 'parents' to spend more time with children, following claims that babies and pre-school children may be disadvantaged if they spend too much time in nursery settings (Mills 2007). However, much of the propaganda and media hype about childhood disorders caused by the lack of quality time with 'parents' is focused only on *mothers'* absences, while fathers continue to be regarded primarily as paternal, economic providers. Richard Collier (1995, 2001) has argued that the emphasis on fathers' identity as 'economic provider' is partly due to the desire of governments and policy makers to impose upon men life-long responsibilities for financial provision for their children, which serves to compound the notion that men who are fathers may well spend quality time with their children, but *only* after they have complied with masculine norms concerning economic provision. Thus, the interpretation of 'masculine' management as commanding, 'being on top of things' (Kerfoot 2000: 232) and spending long hours at work – privileging employment over personal life – puts both male and female managers under pressure.

This chapter has focused on a range of different analyses to explain gendered inequalities in the workplace. It has pointed to a number of different types of inequality and the ways in which feminists and organisational theorists understand the origins and effects of gender and gendering. One of its main aims was to stress that gender does not simply mean 'real' women in the workplace, but refers to a number of ways that people, actions, objects, values, practices, symbols and so on are given gendered values. So far the book has not examined many of the differences between women in much detail, and so the next chapters provide an outline on how differences and inequalities are produced in the workplace, by focusing on race, sexuality and disability in particular. The next chapter specifically looks at how difference has been understood through the lens of what is known as 'diversity'.

MANAGING DIVERSITY: THE TURN FROM EQUAL OPPORTUNITIES

Introduction

In this chapter we map out the concept of diversity in the work-place. The meaning of diversity is much debated, as are the politics of diversity practices. Accordingly, we explore how diversity has been debated, looking at what people see as the pros and the cons of attempting to remedy inequalities and discrimination in the workplace through the concept of diversity. To do this, we examine the relationship between equal opportunities and diversity management. We conclude by looking at the complex work of diversity practitioners.

Defining and Differentiating Diversity and Equal Opportunities

The concept of diversity in the workplace is thought to have originated in the USA, in 1987, with the publication of the report *Workforce 2000* (Johnson and Packer 1987, cited in Litvin 2002). *Workforce 2000* predicted the changing demographics of the labour market in the USA, and speculated on the likely consequences of these changes in relation to the make-up of the workforce (Prasad et al. 1997; Lorbiecki and Jack 2000; Konrad et al. 2006). In the UK, the concept of diversity came to the fore in the 1990s. As several theorists and practitioners have noted, diversity management has now gone global, being used across a number of social domains in Australia, Canada, New Zealand, Scandinavia (see, for example, Litvin 1997, 2002; Prasad and Mills 1997; Konrad et al. 2006; Mir et al. 2006). As the notion of diversity moves to different locations, it takes on new inflections and develops different practices from its North American starting point.

One of the most significant aspects about the term 'diversity' is that, in the workplace, it increasingly eclipses the term 'equal opportunities'. For some, this has meant a rejection of earlier terms used to explore and address discrimination, such as 'equality', 'affirmative action' and 'anti-racism' (Ahmed 2006). Some theorists, for example Jewson and Mason (1994) and Richards (2001), have argued that changes in language reflect a change in approach: over the past thirty years, organisations have shifted from an initial focus on a *social justice* approach to equal opportunities, through to a *business case* approach to equal opportunities and have now shifted to a *managing diversity* approach. As Sara Ahmed and colleagues (Ahmed et al. 2006) suggest, this turn to diversity can mean that other kinds of (perhaps more challenging) vocabularies are no longer central. Thus, terms such as 'equal opportunities', 'social justice', 'anti-racism' and 'multiculturalism' become sidelined. Ahmed et al. (2006) express concerns that, when 'contentious' terms get sidelined, the histories of political movements such as the women's movement and the anti-racist movement might also disappear. They note, for example, that there is little reference made within current policy discussions on equality and diversity to earlier debates on anti-racism versus multiculturalism within education (see Rattansi 1992). Diversity, then, can be seen as potentially depoliticising.

Not only has the term 'diversity' become commonplace – used sometimes on its own and, at other times, paired with the concept of 'equality' – but its take-up is often presented in policy documents and management texts as a uniformly positive move. Cultural theorist Nirmal Puwar observes critically how 'the language of diversity is today embraced as a holy mantra across different sites. We are told that diversity is good for us' (Puwar 2004: 1). Diversity has become 'a ubiquitous and central policy injunction' in schools, health and social care, the private sector, universities (Puwar 2004: 1). Part of this emergence of diversity as an organisational and policy imperative involves an increasing focus on what is referred to as 'celebrating', 'managing' and 'valuing' diversity. This is in distinction from other terms such as promoting equality or fighting racism, which were more prominent in the 1970s and 1980s.

In the public sector, 'diversity' is typically being used by organisations such as public sector organisations, colleges and universities to define their social and educational missions, and their employment practices (Ahmed and Swan 2006). Thus, a further education college may use the term 'diversity' in a range of documents and practices to suggest that it is working to alleviate societal inequalities, to provide working-class, black and minoritised students with qualifications, and to offer its staff equal opportunities in terms of promotions.

In such a wide range of aims, however, the definition of 'diversity' is loose, meaning that it may slip from one connotation to another. The fluidity of the definition of diversity is in some respects problematic, as this may cause anti-discrimination policies to be unspecific (and arguably, thereby, less effective than equal opportunities initiatives). Swan and Hunter (2007) and Sara Ahmed (2006) note that, although it may be more palatable to some managers than the notion of equal opportunities, the word 'diversity' can work to conceal 'the social negatives' of the present inheritance of past inequalities. Examining uses of the term 'diversity' from the perspective of workers with an organisational role to promote diversity, Ahmed (2006) observes how diversity language is experienced as a negative restriction on using a more critical vocabulary. This means that the positive connotations of diversity can function to 'conceal' inequalities from view.

Often, in the UK, 'diversity' is taken to mean 'race' due to the influence of The Race Relations (Amendment) Act 2000. This was a legislative response to the murder of the black teenager Stephen Lawrence that was aimed at tackling institutional racism in the public services. However, diversity is also used as a term to refer to other social groups, such as workers with disabilities. At times it is also used to describe any type of individual difference (for example, interpersonal working style), and changes in recruitment practices and cultural or religious practices. Diversity can be used to describe something that 'individuals' are imagined to have, perhaps linked to particular 'backgrounds', such as gender, race and class but without making them explicit. Its usage can be politically progressive or conservative. Thus, the word 'diversity' is used in such a way that it individuates differences, or it can be used more sociologically to explore structural or group differences rather than imagining difference as belonging to individuals (Kirton and Greene 2004). Diversity can mean different things to different people, representing different types of politics and interests around equality (Omanovic 2006; Swan and Hunter 2007). Diversity, then, is itself diverse!

Equal Opportunities

We now turn to review some of the debates on equal opportunities before examining the politics of diversity in more detail. The term 'equal opportunities' represents a concept which 'is complex, contentious and controversial' (Bagilhole 1997: 29), and it represents a range of debates, theories and practices. One of the core debates is about the nature of equality. There are two influential models in this debate: first, Nick Jewson and David Mason's (1986) distinction between equality of opportunity and equality of outcome, and, secondly, Nancy Fraser's (1997) discussion of equality of redistribution and equality of recognition, both of which we outline below.

We turn first to Jewson and Mason's model, which considers different assumptions about equality and suitable interventions: equality of opportunity or the liberal approach versus equality of outcome or the radical approach. In Jewson and Mason's model, equality of *opportunity* refers to the attempt to offer equal access to services, resources, institutions and social positions via the introduction of fair procedures. In contrast, equality of *outcome* refers to positive action: the provision of differentiated policies to social groups which have been disadvantaged by historical discrimination in order to achieve fair distribution of reward and recognition. This is because the provision of equal access is seen as being insufficient, in itself, to counteract the powerful social structures that have privileged certain groups. Thus, it is argued that 'past disadvantages require us to treat people unequally' (Jencks 1988: 48, cited in Bagilhole 1997: 33). As a result of these different views on equality, different types of organisational practice are seen to ensue.

The liberal approach to equal opportunities (equality of opportunity) is characterised by a belief in the individual, and her imagined abilities and merits, rather than structural sources of inequality. The liberal approach assumes that it is possible to remove the barriers that get in the way of individuals, enabling them to be free to 'make the best of themselves' (Jewson and Mason 1986: 314). The liberal approach is premised upon the idea of fair procedures and sees discrimination as a 'blemish' in that it gets in the way of unfettered competition (Jewson and Mason 1986: 314). The aim of the liberal approach is to create what it sees as equality of treatment in the workplace (Jewson and Mason 1986: 315). This involves eliminating discriminatory procedures and eliminating barriers for individuals. It emphasises bureaucratic formal procedures, such as standardised recruitment and selection, rather than informal approaches (Kirton and Greene 2004). The emphasis is on an *individualised* notion of justice and equality, rather than a group-based justice approach based on the idea of free and equal competition among individuals.

The radical approach to equal opportunities differs from the liberal approach in terms of its understandings and its implications for practice. For one thing, it critiques liberal individualised ideas of 'merit', 'skills', 'talent' and 'ability'. In the radical view, these are socially constructed by those in power and are valued because they are associated with dominant groups (Jewson and Mason 1986: 315). Thus, 'individual merit' is not a neutral term but is a social value judgement that is used to filter out diverse candidates from jobs and promotions. The radical approach to equal opportunities suggests that judgements of skill and talent are based on how closely they fit with the values of white, middle-class men. Unlike the liberal approach, with its individualistic take on inequality and discrimination, the radical perspective on equal opportunities argues that inequality is produced through social norms and practices. Inequality affects individuals but on the basis of their belonging to a social group, for example women, or black and minority ethnic groups. Therefore, the radical approach understands equality as a form of social justice, focusing on monitoring the outcomes of procedures and how they affect different groups. As such, the radical approach is much more interventionist than the liberal approach. In sum, it proposes the equalising of *outcome* rather than of opportunity (Richards 2001: 16). As Jewson and Mason (1986: 315) write, the radical approach holds that 'since it is manifestly the case on *a priori* grounds that women and black people are the equals of men and whites, the actual distribution of occupational rewards should be made to reflect this fact'. Critical of what it sees as the narrowness of the liberal approach, the radical view seeks to politicise the organisation's views and practices so that the unfairness of organisational practices can be seen and addressed.

There are different views on the politics of the liberal and radical approaches to equal opportunities. Cynthia Cockburn (1989) argues that the radical agenda should not simply be seen as the more effective approach. She argues that the radical tactic of positive action – where minority groups are targeted for recruitment, training or promotion – can be counterproductive. In her study, many of the black and women workers she interviewed opposed the idea of positive discrimination: for them, it seemed like favouritism, violating notions of merit and producing backlash from co-workers. As Cockburn (1989: 217) puts it, 'it seeks to put right old wrongs by means that themselves are felt to be wrong'. She also suggests that Jewson and Mason's model is simplistic and rigid: in her view, the needs of employers, managers and minoritised groups are not homogeneous or unified. For her, this means that we need to understand that there are likely to be multiple and competing versions of equal opportunities and disadvantage at any one time. Not all managers think the same way about equal opportunities and not all disadvantaged groups have the same needs.

In sum, Cockburn suggests that both liberal and radical approaches represent 'a strait-jacket we need to break out of' (Cockburn 1989: 215). To do this, Cockburn (1991) proposes that we develop both the short agenda and the long agenda for equal opportunities and see them as different journeys. The short agenda is consonant with the liberal approach outlined above, focusing on eliminating bias in organisational recruitment and promotion practices. The long agenda represents a much more profound transformational project: it involves deeper, radical changes in organisational practices, such as giving minoritised groups access to positions of influence and decision making and resources. For Cockburn, then, the long agenda involves a fundamental changing of the processes by which power is produced and reproduced which she doesn't feel that Jewson and Mason's radical approach addresses.

Having outlined one dominant way of understanding equal opportunities, we now turn to another influential model: Nancy Fraser's model of equality of redistribution and equality of recognition. This brings out a different set of debates around equality. In essence, it focuses on the outcome of moves towards equality and attempts to resolve a split between equality initiatives that emphasise socio-economic outcomes (such as equal access to paid work and education) and equality initiatives which emphasise cultural outcomes. These are more symbolic and include things such as being validated and recognised in society and not being maligned or disparaged through stereotypes in public or in everyday workplace interactions. These two different approaches can lead to different aims, remedies and initiatives to provide economic and cultural justice. Fraser argues, however, that equal opportunities initiatives should not adopt an either/or approach. She makes the point that the economic and the cultural are not 'two airtight separate spheres' but are imbricated or reinforce each other (Fraser 1997: 15). Her view is that, although the aims of redistribution and recognition may be in tension and cause difficulties, minoritised groups need both forms of justice.

For some theorists and practitioners, equal opportunities, regardless of its approach, is fundamentally flawed (Ferreday 2003). This is because of resistance and backlash, some of which is perpetuated by managers. As Linda Dickens (1994, 1999) argues, it is widely believed that 'legislation and corporate policies for promoting equal opportunities have not been effective in eliminating discrimination because they rest on an inadequate perception of the problem, underplay the resistance which equality measures can generate, and simplify the reasons for it' (cited in Lorbiecki 2001: 351). Thus, as Ferreday (2003) suggests, having an equal opportunities policy does not guarantee that an organisation is free from discrimination (Liff 1999; Williams 1999). To the contrary, there is evidence that continuing discrimination '[is] not due simply to misunderstandings or limitations of the policies, but also to deliberate avoidance or distortion by managers' (Liff 1999: 65). As Ferreday (2003) notes, in their 1999 study, Kim Hoque and Michael Noon found that of the top 100 companies they surveyed, those with race equality statements were *more* likely to discriminate against black and minority ethnic applicants than those without. Hoque and Noon (1999: 77) argue that these findings suggest that 'companies were, at worst, using ethnic minority statements as a smokescreen to hide racist practice or, at best, simply paying lip service to equal opportunities'. As a result of various factors discussed above, including the presupposed failure of equal opportunities (EO), diversity management as a concept and set of organisational practices has thus come to the fore.

Managing Diversity

One of the key rationales given for the move to 'managing diversity, is that EO is ineffective because it is divisive and old-fashioned'.

UK human resource management theorists Elizabeth Wilson and Paul Iles (1996: 62) argue that there is a need to move away from EO because it is 'rooted in the social and political agenda of the 1960s and 1970s' and is therefore 'insufficient for the new millennium'. Diversity theorists Raza Mir et al. (2006: 171) put it more critically, arguing that diversity might have been a more attractive concept to employers because it seemed to offer 'analytical categories that were less fractious and potentially divisive than, say, race'. As with equal opportunities, there are different models of diversity and we discuss these below.

For many writers, diversity is thought to derive from two key and contradictory sources: social activism and human resource management. These sources in turn lead to different understandings and agendas. For example, Judith Squires (2003) suggests that where diversity has been influenced by activists, it reflects 'the claims of marginalized cultural groups, social movements, and difference theorists'. But at the same time, diversity also stems from management ideas and is used as a managerial policy and modality of governance' (Squires 2003). These two approaches are often described, respectively, as the 'social justice' and 'business cases' for diversity (Litvin 1997, 2002).

The Business Case for 'Managing Diversity'

The business case for diversity management is related to improving service delivery and economic productivity, and de-politicising models of social relations, a concept which is referred to by Jill Blackmore (2006) as 'capitalizing diversity'. An example of this can be seen in the work of influential diversity consultants Rajvinder Kandola and Johanna Fullerton, who write of the need to 'harness' differences in order to create a productive environment that benefits both the individual and the organisation (Kandola and Fullerton 1994: 8). The business case for diversity presumes that a diverse workforce brings material benefits to an organisation in the form of increased profits, more creativity or more representative customer care. In sum, as Gill Kirton and Anne-Marie Greene (2004) argue, the business case model of diversity involves a rejection of notions of 'justice' in favour of an instrumental, utilitarian model.

For some theorists, the diversity business case is seen to have strategic advantages. For example, Ferreday (2003) outlines the position of Wilson and Iles, who argue that equal opportunities is based on a 'narrow, primarily positivist knowledge base' that constructs organisational culture in the workplace as essentially rational and equitable which, they suggest, is inaccurate (Wilson and Iles 1996: 68). They also claim that equal opportunities is seen by employers as a cost, which means it will meet resistance (1996: 63). As a result, equality activists in the workplace need an approach that will influence management. On this basis, the business case model of diversity is effective because it sees diversity as profitable, and therefore as an investment rather than a cost (1996: 64). This means that the impetus for change will come from within the organisations rather than from outside in the form of legislation, political pressure from government or pushes from social movements. Wilson and Iles argue that equal opportunities approaches see difference as a liability, suggesting that equal opportunities sees the organisational culture as a given that individuals are expected to 'fit into', whereas diversity management 'embraces' difference, seeing it as an asset to the organisation. Wilson and Iles argue that diversity values difference in all its forms (1996: 67). This, they argue, means that the diversity management approach is much less likely to generalise about the needs of people and to conflate different forms of discrimination.

Ferreday (2003) draws on an article by Fondas and Sassalos (2000) to suggest how the business case might operate in the workplace. According to this model, black and minority ethnic women workers bring a variety of different perspectives to their work and the culture of the organisation. This range of perspectives leads to 'richer dialogue, more creative strategic decisions, and better organisational outcomes generally' (Fondas and Sassalos 2000: 13). It is also suggested that these women will be more challenging of taken-for-granted ways of operating within the workplace. Fondas and Sassalos (2000: 14) provide the example of black and minority ethnic women directors, whom they claim are willing to confront poor management decisions and are unlikely to adopt a 'don't rock the boat attitude'. The benefits of the business case are much debated, as is its individuating approach to difference. As Ferreday (2003) notes, in focusing on 'difference' as an individual possession, the collective responsibility of the dominant groups who produce discrimination is sidelined. In the next main section, we consider in more detail the limits of the business case for diversity management. First, however, we observe how the business case model is not the only way of thinking about diversity.

The Social Justice Model for Diversity

Kirton and Greene (2004) argue that it *is* possible to have a more sociological model of diversity management that moves away from the business case model and associated ideas of individuated difference. They argue that it is feasible to have a view of diversity management which favours a structural account of inequality based upon the notion of social justice (Kirton and Greene 2000: 5). For them, diversity management can address the problems of homogenising social groups and their needs, something that is associated with some equal opportunities initiatives.

Kirton and Greene (2000: 4) argue that:

> In our view, the shift away from conceptualising social groups as homogeneous, hermetically sealed units, leads towards a perspective which views social groups as heterogeneous, overlapping and non-fixed. From this perspective a diversity paradigm has the important ability to highlight intra-group as well as inter-group difference, enabling issues of social identity to be drawn out which have been neglected within traditional equality debates.

In this view, the sociological model of diversity management can lead to better equality outcomes for individuals and groups. This is because diversity management emphasises the heterogeneity of difference within social groups. But it does this while holding on to the idea that difference is socially constructed within social relations rather than being an individual possession (Kirton and Greene 2000; Ferreday 2003). This model also moves away from the business case model, which implies that all differences matter equally. The sociological model of managing diversity acknowledges that some differences matter more than others. As research by Ahmed et al. (2006), Hunter and Swan (2007a, 2007b) and others has demonstrated, race and gender have a considerable effect on access to paid work, one's work conditions and experiences, and the likelihood of discrimination.

The Politics of Diversity

As mentioned above, there have been many nuanced and interesting debates on the politics of the 'turn to diversity'. These can be found within organisational theory (Litvin 1997, 2002; Prasad and Mills 1997; Liff 1999; Lorbiecki and Jack 2000; Kirton and Greene 2000; Konrad et al. 2006) and across the social sciences (see, for example, Squires 2003; Cooper 2004; Ahmed and Swan 2006). Below, we provide a summary of some of the key critiques of this turn, and the political issues it generates.

The Language of Diversity

The language of diversity has been seen by some as a more 'palatable' means of promoting equality among employees or dealing with diverse markets than was the language of equal opportunities. In particular, the rise of diversity management has been understood as a direct response to the 'white backlash' against notions of racism and affirmative action (Prasad et al. 1997). As Lowery (1995: 150, cited in Lorbiecki and Jack 2000: 20) argues, 'corporate executives found diversity a lot easier to swallow than affirmative action, and much easier to sell to a predominantly white workforce'. The turn to 'diversity management' which followed has been termed the 'municipal equal opportunities' approach, a perspective which encompassed, for example, terminology such as 'anti-racism' and 'race awareness', especially in public service training. In the late 1980s, in the climate of Thatcherite derision at 'political correctness' and the so-called 'loony-left', such political language was regarded by right-wing commentators as an assault on meritocracy (Walker 2002). Diversity, then, is often presented as a more up-beat, inclusive workplace idea than 'equal opportunities', but 'diversity' may also be welcomed by employers as a less threatening concept than traditional anti-racist activism, which can mean that its effectiveness is diluted.

In a discussion of diversity in urban regeneration in the USA, Gabriella Mogdan (2005) goes as far as to suggest that diversity has become so commodified that it is semantically empty and therefore 'politically bleached'. Ahmed and Swan (2006) also suggest that diversity draws upon particular kinds of vocabulary, which mean that certain terms are no longer used in policy debates, terms such as 'equal opportunities', 'social justice', 'anti-racism' and 'multiculturalism'. These terms are important as they are tied to the history of different political and social movements, such as the women's movement and the anti-racist movement.

Thus they argue that it is striking that there is little reference made within current policy discussions on equality and diversity to earlier debates on anti-racism versus multiculturalism within education (see Rattansi 1992).

Diversity as Excluding

One of the 'selling points' of diversity within organisations has been that it is more inclusive, as it does not claim to focus on any particular social group (Ahmed and Swan 2006). For example, 'diversity' is seen to be, in the words of Thomas, an influential North American Diversity consultant, 'beyond race and gender', and to be about 'everyone' (Thomas 1990). But, as a result, it can negate the specificity of particular experiences, in particular black and minority ethnic women (Thomas 1990). Expanding the term to include wider differences, such as in education, experience, opinions and ideas, can conceal particular forms of inequality that exist within organisations (Benschop 2001). In this view, diversity is paradoxically both 'encompassing and concealing' (Benschop 2001: 1166).

The Limits of the Business Case

There are a number of critiques of the business case approach to diversity. Yvonne Benschop (2001: 1167) notes that hopes that diversity management will 'raise organisational efficiency and effectiveness' may be over-optimistic. Linda Dickens (1994) argues that a business case for diversity can be reversed, and used to *stop* diversity work if diversity proves to be unprofitable or too costly. She goes on to write that business cases are 'invariably contingent, variable, selective and partial' since diversity measures are unlikely to be prioritised in cases where they conflict with what are seen as market pressures (Dickens 1999: 9–10). This can lead to what she calls 'fair weather' equality action (1999: 10). All in all, many theories argue that 'diversity' should be seen as 'an insecure foundation for general overall improvement in the position of women and ethnic minorities' (1999: 9). In this view, diversity needs to be much more closely associated with equality and social justice rather than simply business needs.

Diversity as Image

Diversity is increasingly used as a marketing device, or even as an organisational brand. This is known as the 'glossification' of diversity (Gewirtz et al. 1995, cited in Lingard et al. 2003). One further education college in the UK, for instance, suggests that 'celebrating diversity is second nature to us'. Such statements are typically accompanied by visual images of happy 'colourful' faces, as a visual translation of the diversity metaphor of the so-called multicultural mosaic of Kandola and Fullerton (1994). The inclusion of different faces or bodies in the workplace is imagined to address diversity. As Nirmal Puwar (2004: 1) argues, 'in policy terms, diversity has overwhelmingly to mean the inclusion of people who look different'. But when diversity is seen to be embodied by others, it can allow the whiteness of such organisations to be concealed because the embedded practices, values and cultures of the dominant white group are not counteracted (Ahmed et al. 2006).

'Essential' Differences

Several theorists note the problems when diversity comes to be seen as a property belonging to individuals or groups. Anna Lorbiecki (2001) suggests that many notions of diversity draw on essentialist notions of identity: this means that it is believed that there are universal differences between men and women. For example, it is sometimes imagined that there are 'women's ways' of doing things, such as leading or managing. Even where this is done under the banner of 'valuing diversity' and valuing women's so-called 'special' contribution, this model can perpetuate or even produce inequality rather than bring about equality. This is because the power in producing these types of identity in the workplace is hidden (Lorbiecki 2001: 356–7). In a similar vein, Deborah Litvin (1997: 202) argues that some versions of diversity are essentialist in that they imagine that race, gender and sexuality are 'fixed categories that ... determine who we are'. In her view, this leads to workers being encouraged to see each other as exotic and 'different'. Instead, she suggests that we need to understand how 'difference' is produced through social judgements and social relations in which certain groups have more power to define difference. The powerful can determine who or what is different from whom. According to Litvin, this sets up a 'norm' against which the exotic or different is assessed. In her view, this 'norm' is typically the white male worker. We discuss this idea more in later chapters.

In sum then, as we have seen, the value of diversity is hotly debated among practitioners and academics. And the jury is still out on its efficacy. In any case, regardless of whether initiatives are spearheaded under the auspices of equal opportunities or diversity management, progress in changing the work conditions and experiences of minoritised groups remains painfully slow This raises questions for, and about, practitioners working in the fields of diversity and equality who have to cope with the pros and cons, and tensions and contradictions, of diversity management, and it is to these issues we now turn in the next section.

Diversity Work and Diversity Workers

Although there has been a growing field in diversity critiques, very little has been written on diversity work and diversity workers (see Ahmed et al. 2006; Hunter and Swan, 2007a, 2007b for exceptions). Diversity workers who are 'diversity professionals', in the sense that equality and diversity work is their full-time job, come from different origins. Some were grassroots activists in the 1980s, some have inherited equality and diversity work as part of a wider occupational role and others do diversity work in relation to their position within human resources roles in organisations. In practice, many of the people who do 'diversity work' in a professional capacity are women, and many are from black and minority ethnic groups.

In addition to 'diversity professionals', who are formally involved with diversity management as part of their employment work, many black and minority ethnic workers who are *not* professional diversity workers are also expected to be 'caretakers' of diversity. This is seen to be due to the focus on race in recent equality (Ahmed and Swan 2006). One consequence of this focus is that black and minority ethnic workers are seen as 'signs of diversity … [and] also as responsible for it' (Ahmed and Swan 2006: 3). As black academic Brenda Allen (1995 in Ferreday 2003) notes, this can replace one kind of pressure with another, adding to the workload of black employees. Thus, where black employees were once expected to 'check their race at the door', they now feel under pressure to '"help the organisation" deal with diversity'. Allen notes of her own experience in the workplace that her employers considered it her duty to give 'the minority perspective', to advise white colleagues on how to interact with black students, and generally to offer input on a variety of diversity issues whenever her white colleagues felt they needed it. Doing this did not lead to more pay or status because '[persons] of colour are often expected to fulfil these types of responsibilities, even as they are expected to learn the ropes of their job, and even as others may view them as under-qualified to execute their formal organisational role' (Allen 1995: 150, also cited in Ferreday 2003). In making certain bodies more responsible for diversity than other bodies, the organisation itself is 'let off' from doing this work (Ahmed and Swan 2006). Given that diversity work often has less value than other kinds of work within organisations, being 'stuck with' diversity could become a way in which black and minority ethnic staff get blocked in their careers, doing work that is under-valued and under-resourced. This can lead to increased stress, high workload and poor promotion prospects (Ahmed and Swan 2006).

Documenting Diversity

Professional diversity work includes a range of practices: writing policy documents, providing diversity training to other workers, translating diversity issues for managers, interpreting legislative and policy changes, and trying to get senior commitment to diversity and equality issues. In the UK, the diversity landscape has changed in recent years with the emergence of what Sara Ahmed (2006) calls the 'new equality regimes'. These have had a significant impact on how equality and diversity work is structured, understood and carried out. One of the most significant elements of these new regimes is the Race Relations (Amendment) Act 2000. The Amendment, brought into existence after the murder of the black teenager Stephen Lawrence and the subsequent Macpherson Report (Macpherson 1999), breaks with previous equality legislation through its emphasis on the concept of public duty. This means that public organisations have a specific duty to show how they encourage equality and diversity. This duty is supposed to change the 'burden of proof' for racism (Hunter and Swan 2007a, 2007b). Organisations have to assume race inequality and 'prove' the ways in which they are dealing with this. As a result, public sector organisations are required to publish diversity strategies, race equality action plans, race equality schemes and race equality impact assessments. These structure equality and diversity practices in ways that privilege certain models of race equality (Hunter and Swan 2007a, 2007b).

As a result, producing documents has become a core part of diversity work in the UK. These documents include diversity policies, diversity strategies and action plans, diversity toolkits and checklists, and diversity web pages. These new equality regimes require new skills, tools, analytic frameworks, practices and knowledges in diversity work, such as writing, networking, auditing and monitoring (Kothari 2005). This is also supported through artefacts such as toolkits, data bases, checklists, best practice guides, diversity competences, web pages, academic courses and equality standards – what Uma Kothari calls a 'technocratic and tool-kit approach' (2005: 32; see also Ahmed 2006; Ahmed et al. 2006). Diversity workers are critical of the turn to documents as a major part of their work. As one of Sara Ahmed's (2007) respondents puts it, diversity has become about 'doing the documents and not doing the doing'.

Managing Language and Hiding 'Baggage'

Diversity practitioners are also language workers. This means that they are aware of the politics of words and language around diversity, and use different cases or 'translations' in their work. In a study undertaken by Ahmed et al. (2006), diversity workers showed themselves to be aware of the different ways in which diversity can be conceptualised and presented, and the potential political constraints or trajectories that these may set in motion (Ahmed et al. 2006). They argued that diversity as a concept, while being what they saw as politically constraining, could also be politically energising in a number of ways. For example, in accordance with the views of Bagilhole (1997), they observed how equal opportunities ideas and practices can create confusion, anxiety, anger and suspicion. Barbara Bagilhole (1997: 29) argues that this may be because some members of society (mostly white, non-disabled men) benefit from inequality and may resist equal opportunities policies which appear to threaten the status quo. The 'blankness' of the meaning of diversity was thus seen by diversity practitioners as helpful in three ways. First, diversity as a concept appeared to bring with it what Ahmed calls 'less baggage' than concepts like equality, which have a history of conflict in organisations. Secondly, this lack of 'baggage' meant that diversity could be made appealing to dominant groups. And thirdly, diversity could be used as a kind of 'Trojan horse' to bring in more radical practices such as anti-racism (Jones and Stablein 2006). As a result, some practitioners argued that diversity could be seen as a more positive and celebratory term, which could appeal to different audiences, and thus enable and encourage more people to listen.

One particular tactic that diversity workers used was to draw upon different languages around diversity and around management to get their cases heard. They used the term 'diversity' in different ways and described themselves as 'translators', translating or even 'switching' diversity into different cases for different audiences (Ahmed et al. 2006). For example, some practitioners drew on the business case when discussing diversity with senior managers in the workplace, while defining diversity with a social justice framework for themselves. One practitioner in Ahmed's study (2006) described herself as willing to use any language, including the language of money and compliance, in the interests of addressing inequalities. Ahmed observes, however, that some diversity workers are very critical of the language of diversity management for the same reasons that other practitioners find the term useful.

These various approaches to diversity work put a lot of pressure on diversity workers – not only the diversity 'professionals' but also those staff called upon to do informal diversity work within their organisations. The constant switching between different languages and ideals, the increasing production of documents, the slowness of organisations to change and the work of trying to gain senior management commitment to policy makes diversity work stressful and emotionally draining. Ahmed et al. (2006) argue that the emotional burden of trying to do diversity work, while not being heard (or not being heard in the ways that you want to be heard) is considerable. Diversity work is emotional work which can induce frustration, tiredness and depression due to the feeling that, as one practitioner described, 'you're butting your head against a brick wall'. Overall, Ahmed et al. (2006) argue that diversity work involves the need for complex survival tactics both for professional workers and minority groups called up to do diversity work. These involve extra practical and emotional work which may not be acknowledged, rewarded or supported in the workplace.

In sum, then, the jury is out on the political efficacy of diversity as a concept in the workplace. Some people suggest that diversity is more beneficial as an ideal than equality, but as we shall see in the next chapter, for many minoritised groups, the workplace is still a space of discrimination, violence and oppression. This suggests that we still have a long way to go.

DIFFERENCES AT WORK:
RACE, SEXUALITY AND DISABILITY

Introduction

In this chapter, we discuss race, sexuality and disability. To begin with, we focus on racialisation, racism and racialised practices in organisations, exploring how racial discrimination is produced in organisational and professional processes and practices. We discuss how black and minority ethnic men and women face systematic discrimination in the labour market and the workplace.

We go on to explore the issues for lesbians, gay men and bisexuals in the workplace. We consider the power of universal assumptions that heterosexuality is 'the norm' and the way that these assumptions structure what people think and do. We suggest that heterosexual ideology and discourses permeate all walks of life, including the workplace, meaning that lesbians, gay men and bisexuals (LGB) are often systematically disadvantaged. Finally, we consider the issue of disability and employment. We observe that there have been changes both in policy and approach to disability and paid work which involve an obligation for employers to take practical steps to improve opportunities for those with a disability.

Black and Minority Ethnic Men and Women at Work

Black and minority ethnic men and women still face patterns of inequality, disadvantage and discrimination in the workplace. Research shows the persistence of these patterns. As Nirmal Puwar (2004: 7) writes, 'while the "glass ceiling" has cracked quite significantly in relation to gender, for "race" there exists a "concrete ceiling" [which] has just been chipped ever so slightly'. Karen Proudford and Stella Nkomo (2006) argue that there are still disparities between white and black and minority ethnic workers: in rates of employment; wages, earnings and pay; measures of managerial competence; promotion; exclusion from social networks; access to career opportunities; and in the experience of racisms in their banal and more violent forms.

A number of different statistics on the workplace bear these inequalities out. There is still, over twenty-five years after the introduction of the Race Relations Act in the UK, a stubborn differential between black and minority ethnic men and women's wages, and those of white men and women. For example, the Fawcett Society (2005) published a report on black and minority ethnic women that showed that on average British Pakistani and Bangladeshi women earn only 56 per cent of the average hourly wage of white men. Research by the Cabinet Office Strategy Unit (2003) found that black and minority ethnic workers are also more likely to be unemployed and less likely to have senior positions in management. Worryingly, the Cabinet Office research shows that children of immigrants faced higher unemployment levels in the 1990s than their parents did. A report from 1998 showed that more than 40 per cent of 16 to 17 year olds from black and minority groups were unemployed compared to 18 per cent of their white peers (Penketh 2000: 7). Research by the Runnymede Trust (2006) shows that only 1 per cent of senior managers were from black and minority ethnic groups, even though they make up 7 per cent of the population. This report also showed that in 2005 there were no black and minority ethnic women police chief constables, or judges in the House of Lords or Court of Appeal. There is some progression, in particular for British Indian and African-Caribbean women in terms of salary and occupational status, so there are racialised minorities where they were previously excluded, but progress is slow and uneven across organisations and sectors (Puwar 2004).

The Body Count

The emphasis on the segregation of black and minority ethnic workers in terms of numbers is referred to as the 'body' or 'head count'. But it is only a small part of the story for racially minoritised groups. One of the problems in focusing, through quantitative analysis, on how black and minority ethnic workers are segregated vertically and horizontally in the workplace is that numbers can occlude more subtle processes of racialisation, exclusion and racism.

The 'body count' tends to treat 'gender' and 'race' as variables that can be somehow separated out from the social world. It can help us to understand difference but only as an outcome of bodily characteristics, and not in the context of social relations and meanings (Alvesson and Due Billing 2002). But body counting can produce useful information in relation to wages, positions, occupations, etc. However, it neglects subjectivities, experiences, social processes and practices, and cultural meanings (Alvesson and Due Billing 2002). As Puwar (2004: 32) argues:

> Our analysis needs to go beyond number-crunching exercises which count (monitor) the quantities of different bodies in the stratified structures of institutions. These endeavours are usually based on banal but dominant versions of multiculturalism which assume that the existence of more bodies of colour in the higher ranks of organisations amounts to and is evidence of diversity and equality. The presence of women or 'black' bodies in the upper layers of institutions should not be taken as a straightforward sign that organisational cultures and structures are drastically changing.

The problem with many workplace and policy attempts to diversify organisations is that they focus on getting more black and minority bodies into the workplace (Puwar 2004; Ahmed et al. 2006). The points being emphasised by critical race theorists is that, first, it is not different bodies that make organisations diverse and, secondly, the focus on numbers does not get at the *experience* of black and minority ethnic men and women in the workplace, nor how they are received (Puwar 2004; Ahmed et al. 2006). In focusing on black and minority ethnic workers as embodying diversity, the whiteness of the workplace remains invisible, normative and unchallenged (Ahmed et al. 2006). It is important to note that there are specificities to an analysis of 'race' that make it different from analyses of gender in the workplace. Sometimes it is imagined that race and gender operate in the same ways in organisations and so require the same types of analysis.

In sum, theorists argue that a sole focus on numbers can make genuine change in patterns of inequality much more difficult. For them, the complex processes of racialisation and racism need to be investigated and it is to these issues which we turn next.

Racialisation

The word 'race' is not without controversy as it has a violent history and is associated with discredited views on biological differences between black and white people. Social theorists today argue that 'race' should be understood as a social construction, and so-called racial differences as an invention. In the words of Ali Rattansi (1992: 1), 'no persuasive empirical case has been made for ascribing common psychological, intellectual or moral capacities or characteristics to individuals on the basis of skin colour or physiognomy'. But in spite of being 'invented', 'race' is an organising principle of social life. It divides and categorises people by markers such as skin colour or body type, and so still has conceptual utility. These markers of 'race' supposedly signify underlying essential differences. The division of people into a hierarchy of these differences has a profound effect on people's lives, opportunities, health, and so on (Brah 1992; Proudford and Nkomo 2006: 325). The stubborn, continued existence of race points to 'people's deep social investments in notions of racial difference' (Mac an Ghaill 1999: 4). The concept of race, then, continues to exist more for social reasons than biological ones (Proudford and Nkomo 2006). Theorists argue that race is best understood as an unstable and changing complex of social meanings that organises social relations and meanings (Omi and Winant 1986, cited in Rattansi 1992).

The processes by which race is seen as the key factor in these relations and meanings is referred to as racialisation. Karim Murji and John Solomos (2005) explain that racialisation is used to describe social, cultural, economic and psychological practices that make race significant, put people into racial categories and is used as a basis for exclusion. Although the term is debated, most contemporary critical race theorists argue that racialisation needs to be understood in relation to other social processes of class, gender and sexuality. This means that racism constructs black and minority ethnic men and women differently and does so along class lines. Critical race theorists also argue that race and racialisation should not just be focused on black and minority ethnic people. Thus white people and white bodies should also be conceptualised in terms of race and seen as central to processes of racialisation. As Puwar (2004: 9) puts it, '"race" is seen to reside in minority ethnic men and women' and, at the same time, '"race" is ex-nominated from white bodies, male and female'. White men and women experience their gender, class and sexuality through histories and constructs to do with 'race' as much, albeit on very different terms, as black and minority ethnic men and women. Making whiteness central to racialisation does not mean seeing whiteness as the property of certain bodies. Rather, it is to understand whiteness as part of social relations, something that is reproduced over time through institutional and wider processes, and in changing ways.

Theorising Racialisation

One way to understand racialisation and racism in the workplace is through a materialist perspective focused on capitalist relations (Mac an Ghaill 1999; Rattansi 2005). In this view, capitalist economic processes explain why black and minority ethnic people experience inequalities. Power is seen to be in the hands of institutions, structures and dominant groups and concepts, such as capital, class analysis, state power and institutional structures that are central for understanding racism and racialisation. Thus, British society is understood as 'racially structured' and the most significant aspect of the lack of power for black and minority ethnic groups is their place in the class structure (Mac An Ghaill 1999: 22–5). Hence black labour is best understood as being part of the working class but as being even more exploited than the white working class. Differences between black and minority ethnic groups are seen as secondary to their collective position as a class.

The state is seen as a central player in capitalist relations. In particular, the state's role in encouraging immigrants after the Second World War as a kind of replacement population for the jobs that white people did not want, providing cheap immigrant labour for organisations, is understood as pivotal to this kind of analysis. Black and minority ethnic workers are sometimes understood as an extra type of peripheral workforce – what is called a reserve army of labour – which gets called up and dispensed with according to the vagaries of capitalist dynamics. (In Chapter 3 we noted that this has historically also been the case for women.) Thus, the state is seen as operating on behalf of capital. These theorists argued for a move away from individual and psychologised models of prejudice to an analysis of structural discrimination, produced by powerful institutions in social and cultural life (Mac an Ghaill 1999). These types of study can lead to the impression that the disadvantage and discrimination that black and minority ethnic men and women face in the workplace is due to largely economic reasons.

Black feminists such as Atvar Brah (1996) and Gail Lewis (2000) have argued that these types of theory, which privilege the economic as an explanation for inequalities, neglect other relations. They focus in particular on black women's employment and argue that analyses of racialisation and racism in the workplace need to take account of wider social, political, cultural and discursive formations, and how these affect how black and minority ethnic women are seen, understood, experienced and treated. In bringing cultural issues to bear on these analyses, they also want to move away from simplistic 'culturalist' arguments which explain black and minority ethnic women's differential participation in the labour market to notions of 'ethnic cultures' and their constraining 'norms'. For example, Lewis (2000), in her analysis of how black women were able to enter professional social work, demonstrates the significance of wider issues to do with how black women and families were constructed discursively and socially. In particular, she shows how black families were constructed in policy and the media as 'problems' in need of special expert 'ethnic knowledge' – coming from black women – to help them. At the same time, local authorities had to respond to a range of social movements' demands for social justice and equality, leading to equal opportunities policies in service delivery and employment practices. These discursive constructions and social practices in the 1980s, in her view, made certain kinds of employment possible rather than the economic locations of black and minority ethnic women, as is sometimes emphasised.

Theorists have also begun to counter the model of power in some of the materialist and economic accounts. Rather than emphasising that there is always automatic power for all white people regardless of context or class, they centre their analysis on subjectivity and shifting power relations and the intersections between race, gender, and religious and cultural identities: the lived experience of discourses and representations of race (Brah 1992; Mac an Ghaill 1999; Rattansi 2005). These analyses focus on the interdependencies of race, gender, class and sexuality and show up the contradictions and ambivalence of racism and racialisation. It is argued that there is more to racialisation than simplistic binaries such as black and white, or victim and oppressor. Black and minority ethnic and white groups are not understood as homogeneous or unitary collectivities. There is a greater focus on the differences between black and minority groups and also on the emergence of new forms of racism and ethnicities. As a result, there is a move away from a clear either/or in terms of describing identities, subjectivities, intentions, practices and outcomes as simply racist or non-racist. This does not mean that these theorists want to throw away 'with the bathwater the materialist perspective focusing on capitalist relations and the unequal distribution of economic, political and cultural resources' (Rattansi 2005: 283). Rather, they believe that the operation of racisms and racialisation needs a variety of explanations which do not privilege any one source, location or explanation and show how the economic, social, ideological and cultural are all inextricably intertwined (Brah 1996; Lewis 2000).

Institutional Racism

Some of this complexity has become dulled with the emergence of the concept of institutional racism for understanding mechanisms and processes of exclusion and discrimination in organisations. First used by black academics Stokely Carmichael and Charles Hamilton in the 1960s in the US Black Power movement, the concept of institutional racism differentiated overt, individual racism from covert, institutional practices and non-practices which disadvantage black and minority ethnic men and women (Mac an Ghaill 1999). It was subsequently taken up by social movements, academics and policy makers in the late 1970s, and came to the public fore in the late 1990s with the publication of the Macpherson report in 1999. The term was seen as an improvement on understanding racism in organisations simply as a form of individual prejudice or the product of so-called 'bad apples'. This was because it focused on collective organisational and routine practices and cultures and the way that these, in the words of Macpherson, 'wittingly and unwittingly' produce racist effects for black and minority ethnic employees and service users/customers in the police, hospitals, local authorities and schools, etc. It has since led to much important public discussion, has started to get at the institutional processes of racialisation in public service organisations and has put racism on the workplace agenda in public service organisations.

It has, however, been hotly debated by practitioners, academics and policy makers. Supporters argue that it has moved people away from simply understanding racism as an individual problem of ignorance or prejudice to analysing it as a collective, institutionalised phenomenon that can operate consciously and unconsciously and explicitly and implicitly through systems, procedures and processes. Critics argue that it can give the impression that racism is uniform, ignoring the way that it operates with others forms of differentiation, such as gender, race, class and sexuality (Brah 1996; Rattansi 2005). Rattansi (2005) argues that the concept of institutional racism doesn't emphasise the complex relations that exist between people's identities, their intentions and the subsequent outcomes. All in all, critics feel that other racisms need to be profiled alongside institutional racism so that gendered racisms, national racisms, Jewish racisms, Anti-Arab racism, anti-Irish racism etc. do not get neglected (Brah 1996; Bhavnani 2001). So while the concept of institutional racism has helped complexify our understandings of the origins and operation of racism in the workplace, it is deemed to be too reductionist to work on its own. The next section offers some other ways of understanding racialisation in organisations that can augment the concept of institutional racism in analytically productive ways.

Cultural Cloning in the Workplace

One recent theoretical move to develop more complex understandings of organisational processes and practices of racism and racialisations is to focus on whiteness and normative practices in organisations. For example, according to Philomena Essed, the concept of diversity in the workplace focuses too much on those constructed as 'different'. Thus, she argues that it 'lets off the hook the normative practices [and] business continues as usual' (Essed

2005: 228). Diversity becomes interpreted as having to deal with, in her words, 'something extra' and not the 'same and not the familiar business as usual' (2005: 231). In her view, a more useful approach is to examine 'cultural cloning' processes in organisations which hold up certain groups as the norm. What she means by cultural cloning is the way that gate-keeping processes are used in organisations to select individuals. In particular, they are used to recruit people who are seen as 'like-minded, like-looking, like family, like "us"' (2005: 229). As a result, they can ensure an imagined homogeneity in the workforce, particularly in senior positions (2005: 228). These gate-keeping processes include 'networks of patronage' (Back et al. 2001: 37). Cultural cloning, in this view, is a preference for the same type of person in organisations. Usually, Essed suggests, this type is a combination of 'masculinity, whiteness, European-ness, able-bodied-ness' and is based on normative judgements of competence and values (Essed 2005: 229). These values are racialised and gendered, and reproduced through local situational processes in the work-place, on and off the job. Like Gail Lewis, Essed argues that organisational practices are given their impetus and power by wider cultural, political and social practices and formations: what she refers to as a 'larger package of norms, values and practices' (Essed 2005: 244). Overall, the aim of cultural cloning, she argues, is to enable dominant groups to secure 'spaces of privilege' (2005: 243).

Taking the Dutch medical profession as her case study, she argues that there are three modes of sustaining whiteness in this profession. The first of these is what she terms the over-representation of masculine mentors. This refers to the dominance, in numbers and values, of white men in the medical profession. This dominance maintains a cultural climate, in her view, which reinforces western, masculine values and practices. The second factor is everyday racism as a mode of white identification. For Essed, this refers to recurring but accumulative racist incidents such as being put down, rejected, ignored, being joked about, which undermine black and minority ethnic women and men's confidence. In addition, these apparently trivial incidents become a mechanism for bonding between white middle-class men, reaffirming whiteness as the norm. The third mechanism in her case study is the privileging and rewarding of masculine and white cultural values in the medical profession. As a result, alternative ways of doing things are marginalised, trivialised or ridiculed. In her view, the concept of cloning cultures and practices enables a more sophisticated analysis of the workplace and the way that they reproduce certain norms and values in the workplace.

The Somatic Ideal

Essed's analysis looks at how occupations and workplaces keep black and minority ethnic people *out*. By contrast, in a UK-based study of MPs and senior civil servants, Nirmal Puwar (2004, whose work we also discuss in Chapter 5, in relation to gender), examines what happens when black and minority ethnic men and women get *in* to the workplace. Referring to these groups as 'space invaders', she investigates what happens to minoritised groups when they are employed in places from which they have previously been excluded. Puwar examines the contradictory terms by which minoritised groups are received by white men in Parliament and the senior civil service. In her analysis, Puwar emphasises the importance of the body, which is seen as central to reproducing ideas about what is 'the norm', the 'proper', appropriate way to be and to behave in the workplace. Puwar describes this idea of the normal worker's body as 'the somatic ideal'. Even though her focus is on the body, she is keen to stress the way in which the 'somatic ideal' of whiteness and middle-class masculinity is reproduced and circulated through practices, systems, representations, customs, and behaviour within these organisations. Thus, she writes, 'whiteness and masculinity are embedded in the character and life of organisations' (Puwar 2004: 32), adding that 'the timing, working procedures, rituals and bodily performances endorse specifically classed notions of masculine Englishness' (2004: 36). As a result, black workers are required to 'whitewash' gestures, speech patterns, interests and value systems in order to conform to the behavioural 'norms' of the workplace. Whiteness, then, is an ongoing process which continually reproduces the somatic norm as its ideal worker: it is not simply a given. Puwar's work emphasises how the specific history, class and context of a workplace can produce particular racialised processes.

In a different example, Les Back and colleagues look at the particular racialised processes in football occupations and organisations. These include the creation of a certain type of racist who is constructed as responsible for all racism in football. They refer to this as the 'identikit' racist. This is where racism is attributed to a few individual fans or so-called 'bad apples' so that a distinction can be made between the 'mindless minority' and the so-called 'normal, respectable' fans (Back et al. 2001: 164). Focusing on the mindless minority fans also moves attention from everyday banal and casual institutional processes, structures, cultures and language which normalise whiteness and militate against black and minority ethnic interests within football institutions. Back and colleagues show how these constructions of the racist hooligan are classed, and add that we need to 'remain critical of the ideological processes which organise racism simultaneously into the bodies of deviant white working-class men and out of the middle-class professional spheres where racism and racial inequality possess more genteel manners' (Back et al. 2001: 284). In their view, this classed presentation of the hooligan racist fan isolates racism from institutional commercial and human resource interests so that they can adopt a colour-blind philosophy. This supposed colour-blind approach cannot attest to the presence of racism with the institutional and middle-class management processes and structures. Thus, the predominance of white professionals in football management, the networks of white patronage, the forms of stereotyping that fix attributes of black and white players which reproduce the view that black players can't be managers, and the informal white-centred environments in which job opportunities are shared are never discussed. As a result, everyday casual forms of racism can be dismissed as humour, a wind-up. All in all, these racialised and racist processes lead to what they refer to as 'out-thereism', where racism is attributed to someone or somewhere else (Back et al. 2001: 194).

Puwar also discusses the problem of organisations imagining themselves as colour blind. She argues that in this approach, any differences should not be mentioned because we should all be seen as the same. This means that anyone noting differences is seen as 'making things worse'. As a result, black and minority ethnic women and men can be seen as trouble-makers, people who are too disruptive. As Sara Ahmed et al. (2006) comment, being a black and minority ethnic worker and getting involved in 'anti-racist' work is risky. They write that 'whilst you can "embody" diversity, by adding colour to the organisation, to speak out about racism can "re-mark" you as a source of institutional trouble' (Ahmed et al. 2006: 81). In the move to get more 'diversity', organisations recruit black and minority ethnic workers, expect them to take an interest in (if not responsibility for) 'diversity' programmes (see Chapter 4) and then require them not to be 'too black' or too truthful about the whiteness they encounter. Paradoxically, diversity, as is currently practised in workplaces, seems to be about sustaining whiteness.

At the same time as outlining racial discrimination and racist processes, it is important to recognise the persistence of black and minority ethnic workers' coping and resistance strategies in the workplace and wider society. The recognition of these strategies can stop black and minority ethnic women and men being seen as 'passive victims' while still acknowledging the systematic and complex operation of racisms, discrimination and inequalities that are perpetuated in the workplace and other social institutions. As well as early organised bodies such as the Campaign for Racial Discrimination, set up in 1964, there were grassroots and community groups such as the Indian Workers' Association Southall, the British Caribbean Association, the National Federation of Pakistani Associations and the Council of African Organisations; the Black Power Movement, Black Unity and the Racial Adjustment Action Society in the late 1960s and early 1970s, and Asian Feminist and Youth Movements in the mid-1970s, such as Black Southall Sisters (Lent 2001). Many major industrial strikes, such as those at Grunwick and Imperial Typewriters in the 1970s, were led by South Asian men and women, for example Jaya Ben Patel, to fight for better working conditions (Brah 1996). In more recent years, black staff networks have been set up in workplaces, for example the Network for Black Managers in Further Education, to provide support and advice for black and minority ethnic workers. There are, then, other inequality fighting practices in addition to those formally institutionalised by workplaces, created and run by black and minority groups themselves.

In sum, this section has shown different analyses of how racialised relations take place in the workplace. As with feminist accounts of gender, critical race theorists draw upon a range of different types of analysis, including the materialist and the cultural. There is also a growing field of study of organisational practices and processes which is developing a nuanced theory of how racisms and racialisation operates through the everyday.

Sexuality

> We inhale heterosexuality with the air we breathe. This is really what is meant by institutionalised heterosexuality or heterosexuality as a site of power. (Dunphy 2000, cited in Carabine 2004: 17)

This quote from a social theorist of sexualities emphasises the extent to which heterosexuality is seen as 'the norm'. The quote also stresses the powerfulness of heterosexual ideals – in which everyone is assumed to be universally heterosexual – and the way that these ideals structure people's thoughts and behaviour. As a result of the way that heterosexual ideology and discourses permeate all walks of life, including the workplace, lesbians, gay men, bisexuals and trans individuals (trans referring to transgender, transsexual, transvestite) (LGBT) may be systematically disadvantaged and discriminated against. They may have unequal access to employment benefits, are often denied promotion and career advancement, and may be subject to harassment, persecution and violence (Oerton 1996; Humphrey 1999; Creed 2006). This is in spite of the fact that what constitutes 'normal' sexuality is contested, and the meanings attached to sexual acts, relationships, practices and identities are complex and contradictory (Carabine 2004: 2).

Stonewall, one of the campaigning organisations for LGBT, contends that research consistently shows that discrimination and harassment are serious problems for LGBT in the workplace. They cite a study by the TUC (1999) in which, out of some 450 lesbian, gay or bisexual trade unionists, 44 per cent reported that they had suffered discrimination due to their sexuality. In the worst cases, this involved dismissal, but a significant number reported instances of derision, and homophobic abuse. In a more recent Unison survey (2003) over 52 per cent said that they had been discriminated against because of their sexual orientation (cited in Colgan et al. 2007).

Sociologist Jill Humphrey's 1999 study of 23 lesbian and gay men working in a trade union showed a range of the outcomes of workplace discrimination: three had been discharged from the military, three were 'outed' in the tabloid press and retired as a result, one lesbian transferred due to persecution, or what Humphrey refers to as 'lesophobia', and one gay man had been dismissed as a result of his colleagues' homophobic beliefs about AIDS. Several of her interviewees suspected that they had not been offered jobs as a result of their sexual identities.

In a more recent report published in 2007 on lesbian, gay and bisexual workers, Fiona Colgan and colleagues suggest that one in five of respondents said that they had experienced discrimination on grounds of their sexuality in the past five years. Experiences included ostracism by colleagues, homophobic comments and insults, discomfort and embarrassment caused by the negative attitudes and behaviours of managers and colleagues, and bullying and physical intimidation.

In the past five years, there has been an increase in legislation around sexuality and transgender equality. This includes the Employment Equalities (Sexual Orientation) Regulations (2003), the Gender Recognition Bill (2003) and the Civil Partnerships Bill (2004). But in spite of this legislation and nearly thirty years of campaigning by lesbian and gay men, systematic inequalities remain, and sexualities and transgender equality work is unevenly carried out (Humphrey 1999; Monro 2007). Surji Monro (2007) argues that some public services organisations have taken up the rhetoric of sexualities and transgender equality in order to be seen as progressive and active, while not making many practical changes at the level of service provision for customers and clients. Overall progress remains slow and LGBT can experience discrimination, persecution and even violence in the workplace, as the studies cited above show.

It is also important to note that LGBT workers can have very different experiences of sexual discrimination from women, disabled workers or racialised minorities. This is because ideas about heterosexuality are affected by other discourses on able-bodiedness, race, gender and age. For example, Jean Carabine argues that racialised ideas have constructed black and Asian women and men – albeit in different ways – as closer to nature, lacking sexual control, erotic, exotic and hyper-sexed (Carabine 2004: 8). She adds that disabled men and women are seen as incapable of sex, without sexuality and as sexually vulnerable (Carabine 2004).

So, although LGBT can be on the receiving end of hate and disgust in the workplace, referred to as homophobia, the type and form of homophobia can vary according to gender, 'race', fears about AIDS, self-presentation, etc. (Humphrey 1999). Carabine argues that one of the main barriers to change in the workplace and wider society is the presumed 'normality' and appropriateness of heterosexuality. Thus:

> It is commonly assumed that most people will be heterosexual and we take for granted as natural and normal that people will be attracted to someone of the opposite sex ... [and that it is] natural for men and women to get married or live in a monogamous heterosexual relationship. (Carabine 2004: 7)

This 'normalisation' of heterosexuality leads to the normalisation of marriage and the 'nuclear' family: what theorists call 'heteronorma- tivity'. Thus, marriage becomes the 'preferred social arrangement for partnering and parenting, which is privileged over and above other arrangements such as same-sex or cohabiting heterosexual partnerships' (Carabine 2004: 13). Heteronormativity is about social and cultural processes which maintain and circulate the idea that heterosexuality is normal, universal and natural. Heteronormativity operates within organisational and management theory and research. For example, Gillian Dunne (1998) notes how it is typically assumed that workers, parents and households are heterosexual in much contemporary theory on the workplace. Where lesbians are taken into account, she argues, they are assumed to mirror heterosexual practices in relation to housework and parenting. In her view, sexual identity is important for under- standing people's experience of work. Dunne (2000) suggests that research on lesbian experience can provide new insights on theo- rising work and family life. Overall, there is still a neglect of LGBT workplace experiences in organisational and management theory (Oerton 1996).

Heteronormativity is understood, however, as institutionalised. Although normalisation operates at the level of an individual's attitudes and belief, theorists are keen to emphasise the way that heteronormativity is embedded, reproduced and sanctioned through social institutions such as the law, government, education and culture. In this view, institutional heterosexuality shapes personal relationships and individual practices but also organises wider social relations, practices and institutions and the policing of sexual identities (Dunne 2000; Carabine 2004). And through these, heterosexuality is constructed as universal, stable, natural and fixed while other forms of sexuality are seen as 'other'. Heterosexuality is not only a means of organising the personal and public world, but it is also a site of power, inequality and privilege (Carabine 2004: 16). Heterosexuality is not simply about so-called private life, but shapes 'everyday life though the social institutions and social practices of marriage, reproduction and parenting' (2004: 10). At the same time, heteronormativity is continuously contested because the meaning of sexuality and sexual identity are not settled. But this also means that sexuality and sexual identities are intensely regulated and surveilled.

Institutional heterosexuality operates within the workplace at different levels: in interactions, practices, discourses, stories, norms, policies, etc. These can operate on an everyday, taken-for-granted basis, as Robyn Wiegman's (2000) account of social interactions in a workplace suggest. Wiegman (2000: 73) argues that 'heterosexual marriage, family, and reproduction … [structure] the interpersonal codes, affective economies, and social practices' on an everyday basis. To demonstrate this point, Wiegman provides examples of social interactions between colleagues, where the assumption is made that everyone is heterosexual, married and with children. Her point is not simply that lesbians, gay men, and bisexuals can't join in. It is that this workplace – in her case, a university – organises itself as what she calls 'a social community' through heteronormative practices and assumptions about how many children you have and the gender of your partner (2000: 73). Wiegman refers to the 'everyday constellation of heterosexual reproductive forms and social practices' (2000: 74), which includes practices such as the decoration of offices with family photos. Such apparently mundane activities, she suggests, 'dictate appropriate sociality' but also emphasise the everyday, practical level at which heterofamilial ideals are reproduced (2000: 73–5). What Wiegman terms 'everyday protocols' in the workplace thus regulate, and regularise, relationships in the workplace through notions of the 'normative' relationship or family form. Again, the everyday and banal can be seen to reproduce inequality and discrimination.

Heterofamiliality at work makes if difficult for the lesbian, gay man or bisexual to have a 'public narrative' of their private life (Wiegman 2000: 78). As a result, LGBT lack status as mother or spouse within the norms of institutional sociality because their life or identity outside the workplace may not be recognisable among colleagues, thus making LGBT feel pressured to keep their partners secret. In this way, lesbian, gay and bisexual existence is erased from the workplace (Adkins 1995). This censoring and lack of recognition could be seen to exemplify Nancy Fraser's (1997) influential distinction between equality of recognition and equality of distribution discussed in Chapter 4. Equality of recognition addresses issues to do with status inequality and lack of cultural recognition. The latter is to do with the redistribution of economic and material resources.

It might be seen that Wiegman's experiences fit in with the cultural equality of recognition. But this would be to ignore the inequalities of economic and material resources that come with lack of recognition and the way that the political economy is imbricated in culture and vice versa, as the following discussion shows (Duggan 2003).

Some lesbians, gay men and bisexuals try to counter the erasure of their sexual identity through 'coming out', that is letting people know about their identity. Some LGBT feel that living the lie – not being true about one's identity or lifestyle, fearing the spread of rumours or being 'discovered', and struggling to pass as heterosexual or to maintain different lifestyles at work and at home – means that coming out is not really a choice but an inevitability (Humphrey 1999; Colgan et al. 2007; Creed 2006). However, this is not an easy option, nor is it without danger. As Douglas Creed (2006: 379) puts it, 'coming out is perhaps the *sin qua non* of LGB emancipation but it also increases the likelihood of being the target of discrimination' in the workplace. Coming out can lead to harassment, pay discrimination, denial of promotion, ostracism, job loss and even physical violence. Respondents in Colgan et al.'s (2007) study said that fears about career progression, lack of visible senior LGBT staff, previous negative experience of discrimination and harassment, macho attitudes and religious attitudes of co-workers and respecting a partner's wishes were all reasons that prevented them coming out. Stonewall suggest that most workers stay 'in the closet' to avoid discrimination and persecution, fearing that this would be the result if they were to come out.

As many theorists note, coming out is not a one-off event. It is an ongoing process of decision making. As Creed (2006: 379) writes, 'each and every work relationship may entail a new and potentially difficult disclosure'. The expectation of being out all the time can be exhausting (Wiegman 2000). The decision is not simply one of telling people either, but involves dilemmas about whether and how to claim one's sexual identity (Creed 2006). For example, respondents in the research by Colgan et al. (2007) used a variety of tactics for coming out over a period of time, including coming out to individual colleagues, referring to a same-sex partner, making references to gay issues in workplace conversations, and displaying photos of partners. The process of coming out can also be tortuous, as Humphrey (1999) notes, adding that coming out can mark a point of no return. Colgan et al. (2007) showed that some LGBT workers felt able to come out early in their careers when their organisations followed LGBT equalities initiatives and had what they called a 'gay friendly' environment. However, black and minority ethnic, and disabled LGBT respondents in the study reported multiple discrimination as a result of racism, disable-ism and homophobia. As a result, some in these groups said it was easier not to come out about their sexuality. For some respondents, coming out was a painful and uncomfortable experience, leading to exclusion and harassment (Colgan et al. 2007).

Being 'out' can also mean having to be an expert on sexuality. As Humphrey (1999: 134) writes, 'those who dare come out will tread a precarious tightrope between being out and pursued for their specialist knowledges, and out and persecuted'. Thus LGBT in the workplace are often assumed to know about all 'non-heterosexual' sexualities and are asked to address all issues to do with sexual questions. It can also mean being caught up in social pressure to be a 'good gay', as opposed to a 'bad gay'. 'Good gays' are seen as acceptable because they are in stable, monogamous relationships and don't flaunt their sexuality. '"Bad gays" are "in your face" raging queens or queers, who engage in unsafe sexual practices', don't act heterosexual enough and are deemed too sex-ually perverse' (Carabine 2004: 39). The normalising of the 'good gay' – the heterosexual-friendly version of homosexuality – has been referred to as a 'new homonormativity' (Duggan 2003: 50). This 'good gay' is seen to uphold heteronormative practices, assumptions and institutions by keeping gay culture private and de-politicised. In Warner's view (1999), the idea of the 'good gay' takes the sexual out of homosexual by domesticating it for heterosexual culture.

LGBT end-users, customers and clients can all suffer as a result of the heteronormative culture of the workplace. Their sexuality can be denied or misinterpreted. For example, sexuality may be understood as a sexual practice, rather than as also being about relationships, intimacy and identity (Carabine 2004). Equally, LGBT professional workers experience problems. Lesbian and gay welfare professionals can feel vulnerable about being 'out' at work, particularly when their role involves working with children or the provision of intimate care (Carabine 2004; Creed 2006). This is because a wider set of cultural discourses conflate homosexual-ity, perversity and paedophilia, leading to constructions of the depraved and diseased homosexual who is unfit for working with children in the role of teacher, social worker or nursery nurse (Humphrey 1999; Creed 2006). In this context, it is imagined that the so-called homosexual 'lifestyle' (associated with drug abuse, obsession with sex and unsafe sexual practices) is contagious, and will become normalised and taken up by children, thus putting their safety and well-being at risk (Creed 2006).

In spite of the difficulties and problems, many LGBT workers have a range of strategies for dealing with heteronormativity and homophobia at work. For example, in Colgan et al.'s (2007) study, respondents described a range of responses and tactics for coping with discrimination, harassment and discriminatory attitudes. These include using humour, ignoring remarks, hiding emotion and more head-on strategies such as directly challenging prejudice, seeking to educate people and taking control of situations. Forms of support drawn upon by LGBT workers included sympathetic line managers, trade unions, LGBT groups and networks, equalities units, colleagues, friends and employee counselling services. Being part of LGBT groups and networks enabled respondents to socialise with LGBT colleagues, to find and give support, and to campaign and negotiate on LGBT issues.

Having outlined a number of issues around sexuality and heteronormativity in the workplace, the chapter finishes by considering the issue of disability.

Disability

What about disabled workers? Since 1995, when the Disability Discrimination Act became law (Kirton and Greene 2000), there have been changes to employment policy in relation to disability and paid work. Much of the impetus for this came from the lobbying of the disabled people's movement. Work and employment have been a key concern for this group since the 1970s due to the effects of a lack of employment on poverty and the exclusion of people with disabilities (Barnes 2000). Many of these policy changes oblige employers to take practical steps to improve opportunities for those with a disability. The 1995 Disability Discrimination Act, and the changes it has subsequently imposed upon organisations, has reflected a change in the social understanding of disability. Prior to 1995, the 'medical model of disability' was the most common frame of reference for policy makers, employers and organisations to apply to disability. The individualised medical model of disability constructed disabled people as 'problems'. The negative approach to disability which the medical model encapsulated was reflected in the treatment of disabled staff by employers. People with a disability were, therefore, often regarded by employers as unproductive and problematic in comparison with able-bodied people.

One key purpose of the disability movement is to change the way that disability is understood, and to move from a 'bio-medical' to a 'social' approach, with the intention that this will improve the treatment of disabled people in society. Alongside disabled activists, scholars such as Thomas (2007) and Woodhams and Corby (2003) have worked towards challenging bio-medical definitions of disability. In this view, disability is not a medical condition, but a socially constructed concept formed on the basis of a narrow social viewpoint about what is 'normal' and about how particular social and organisational tasks should be performed. In essence, it looks at how society is disabling, focusing on how social, cultural and environmental factors disable and marginalise people with impairments. Thomas (2007) notes how disabled women are often judged primarily in terms of their disability and are thus discounted from being able to fulfil social roles because others consider only what they are *not* able to do, as opposed to foregrounding the competencies of disabled women. Thomas criticises the bio-medical definition of the disabled body as being somehow lacking or less effective than an able body. Thomas thus argues for a 'social' model of disability, whereby workplace and other public spaces are re-ordered so as to accommodate a variety of needs.

In accordance with Thomas, the Disability Rights Commission (DRC) argues how 'the Social Model of Disability is an alternative way of understanding access issues and social exclusion and sees the problem as a "disabling world"' (DRC *c.* 2004). The DRC challenges the barriers faced by many disabled people and argues that society must change in order to better and more fairly facilitate the participation of disabled people. The DRC promotes the need for 'consulting with disabled people, changing attitudes, policies and practices, rethinking budget priorities and expenditure, and exploring why our society doesn't treat all its members as equal (DRC *c.* 2004, inserted leaflet on Medical and Social Models of Disability).

Since 1995, in keeping with the aims of the DRC, employers have been compelled to think about how they can offer better facilities for those with a disability to participate equally in activities. From October 2004, the laws on disability and employment became more focused and it is now unlawful for any UK employer to discriminate against a disabled person in the recruitment process, either in terms and conditions of employment, or in relation to promotion and/or by treating disabled staff unfairly in comparison with colleagues. Disability laws reach out to include government agency and public organisations in their remit, so, for example, religious organisations with public meeting places are also encouraged to think about how they can better accommodate disabled members – and to act upon this.

Employers are now obliged to consider how they can attract and retain disabled staff and how they can integrate and retain workers who become disabled during the course of their employment. Organisations are required by law to make 'reasonable adjustments for disabled job applicants and/or disabled staff when a provision, criteria or practice ... or a physical feature of their premises, puts a disabled person at a substantial disadvantage' (Disability Rights Commission c. 2004). 'Reasonable adjustment' can be interpreted broadly, and might include altering a person's working hours, acquiring special equipment, allowing absences for medical or therapeutic appointments, providing additional supervision and making physical adjustments to premises. These requirements affect not only corporate and public institutions, but also small businesses such as corner shops. The Disability Rights Commission has pointed out that employers' fears relating to the financial implications of employing disabled people (for example, making alterations to workplace premises) are often out of all proportion to the actual cost of such provisions. The DRC note that 'reasonable adjustment' often costs very little, and might mean simply rearranging workplace layouts to accommodate staff with disabilities. Even if money does have to be spent, the DRC observed that, in 2004, the average cost of this was low, and was likely to be only around £75.00 (DRC c. 2004).

Yet in spite of these legislative moves, there is still profound 'disabilism' and institutional discrimination encountered by people with disabilities in the workplace. Disabilities academic, Colin Barnes (2000: 445) sums it up by saying 'there is universal agreement that disabled people are disproportionately disadvantaged in the current labour market'. People with disabilities are much more likely to be unemployed or under-employed than the general population, less likely to be employed in visible customer-facing roles, more likely to have their work capabilities underestimated, more likely to be seen as less dependable workers, and more likely to be seen as not being able to get along or be accepted by other workers than their contemporaries (Jackson et al. 2000). They are also not promoted as often as their non-disabled colleagues.

One of the main problems for activists and theorists with the Disability Discrimination Act (DDA) is that it returns to an individualised model of disability. This means that the individual's disability is seen as the problem rather than the disabling environment and practices of the workplace. The Act also puts the onus on the individual to raise issues about the workplace. Recent research suggests that rather than addressing inequalities in the workplace, the DDA individualises disability, focusing on personal impairment as opposed to questioning the whole concept of "disability" *per se*' (Thomas 2007: 12, emphasis in original). Yet again, we see how legislation on its own cannot address social, economic and cultural issues in the workplace which produce inequality and discrimination.

In sum, this chapter has examined three significant social relations – racialisation, sexuality and disability – which lead to unequal and oppressive practices in the workplace. These three aspects have their own specific processes, histories, contexts and forms of discrimination. They also work together in complex ways, which we discuss in our next and final chapter.

6

CONCLUSION: FROM THEORY TO PRACTICE?

At the beginning of this text, we asked the question: 'Why do we need a book entitled *Gender and Diversity in Management?*' We suggested that one reason for writing the book was that, despite legislation and the hard work of campaigning organisations such as the Equal Opportunities Commission, discrimination remains widespread and persistent. This may be partly because, as Barbara Bagilhole (1997) argues, the notion of 'equal opportunities' ideas and practices often creates confusion, anger and suspicion. Bagilhole further argues that some members of society who have already benefited from inequality – usually white, non-disabled men – may resist equal opportunities policies, especially if they feel that their opportunities and prospects are threatened as a result (1997: 29).

Equality, then, in terms of both ideas and practices has come to be seen as what Sara Ahmed calls 'worrying', being associated with the law, legislation, restrictions and threats and thus making individuals and organisations feel defensive. With particular reference to minoritised groups, we have already acknowledged that, for these reasons, the notion of 'diversity' may in some respects be helpful because it carries less baggage and has a more positive image than 'equal opportunities'. For some practitioners and academics, the celebratory feel and the newness of diversity compared with equal opportunities is thus useful. Ahmed et al. (2006), and Swan and Hunter (2007) have argued that the vagueness of the meaning of diversity accounts for its increased use in the workplace. This accords with research by Ahmed et al. (2006), which shows that the fluidity associated with the notion of diversity can be appealing to employers and politically enabling for diversity workers.

Conversely, however, for the same reasons that practitioners sometimes find the term useful, many of those working in the diversity field are also very critical of the notion of 'diversity' because, as Ahmed et al. (2006) observe, the appeal of diversity comes with its own limitations and costs. There is, however, continued and sustained evidence that minoritised groups still experience much discrimination, inequality, oppression and violence in the workplace.

What about gender? At the start of Chapter 2, we examined the idea that 'it's all gone too far', and we challenged assumptions that women's rights 'have been achieved'. As we penned the conclusions to this book, we were presented with some convincing evidence that, for some who hold the most influential positions in society, the notion of equal opportunities for women and the laws which are supposed to protect women's rights appear to be an irrelevance. When it comes to television, and multi-million pound business, it seems to us that it is possible for those who hold powerful roles in society to flout the law, without charge, and in the most public arena possible.

In the summer of 2007, the UK version of *The Apprentice* televised a series of interviews in which finalists of a competition (the winner of which would be offered a 'top job' as 'the Apprentice' to UK businessman Sir Alan Sugar) were 'grilled'. Of the five contestants, two were women. In the women's interviews it was acknowledged that both candidates were quite capable of doing the job on offer. Once this was established, the questions put to the women seemed to focus almost entirely on the women's ability (or otherwise) to combine childcare responsibilities with paid work. Finally, after gruelling questions from Sir Alan Sugar, the Chief Executive of the company offering the job, about whether she could care for her two young children *and* fulfil the role of 'Apprentice', Katie, one of the leading job candidates, pulled out. The programme was aired at peak viewing time to an audience of several million. This suggests that the television and business executives involved in the competition assumed that equal opportunities legislation did not apply to them, and that they were somehow justified in their approach. Apparently, they felt sufficiently confident to air, on prime time television, the kind of discriminatory exchange which legislators, feminists and campaigners have fought for years to stamp out (Gatrell 2005).

It seems extraordinary (and disheartening) that, over thirty years since the enactment of sex discrimination laws, the male finalists on *The Apprentice* were interviewed principally on their ability to do the job, while the women were still judged primarily on the basis of whether childcare responsibilities might make them unreliable and uncommitted employees. Furthermore, it was discouraging to observe how neither female candidate seemed to feel enabled to rule such questions 'out of order', on the grounds of their irrelevance and probable illegality. Both women answered the questions directly, one candidate attempting to convince interviewers that she could manage both her son and her job, the other woman (Katie) appearing to suffer a complete crisis of confidence, meaning that she was pushed to the sidelines and out of the race. Thus, there remains a need for continued debate on gender and diversity in management. There is still ongoing unequal treatment of individuals and groups built into organisational practices, cultures, discourses and policies.

Our final conclusion is around inter-sectionality. One of the problems in separating out gender from other social categories, such as class, race, age etc., is that it neglects the differences between women. It also ignores the way that gender, sexuality, age, class and race all operate with and through each other: we should not understand them as separate processes or spheres. As such, these interrelations need to be brought together much more so that we understand the complex ways in which gender operates and the ways that inequality is differentially formed and experienced. Thus, women do not experience discrimination solely on the basis of gender; they may also experience it on the basis of class, age, sexuality, ethnicity, race, religion, and disability. For example, black disabled people are subject to unique forms of discrimination which are different from the adding together of racism as a black person and disablism as a disabled person (Swain et al. 2003).

These social relations also interact. This means that racism and classism operate together, producing complex and multiple intersections, oppression and inequalities. In this view, we cannot isolate one single source or origin of oppression. But this is more than an additive model of discrimination, that is, where you layer one inequality on top of another. Rather, inter-sectionality means that social relations operate simultaneously and do so at multiple levels: at cultural, economic and social levels through social policy, the legal system, cultural representations, education, but also at the personal experiential level (Chancer and Watkins 2006).

These operations of inter-sectionality have been ignored in much organisational theory. Hence, while there has been an increase in literature on women in the workplace in recent management and organisational theory, much of this assumes a white, heterosexual, able-bodied, middle-class career woman. The universalism of these gendered models is often not questioned and, thus, the quite different experiences of different women are occluded. This is not to say that there cannot be some commonality or common ground between women (Chancer and Watkins 2006), but it is important to recognise that inequalities, oppression and discrimination in the workplace do not operate in the same way on all women. In separating out different social relations – gendering, racialisation, sexuality, disability – in this book, we have wanted to highlight the different types of theory about, histories of, and experiences of inequality in the workplace. However, at some point, the ways in which these operate together need to be thought through in future management and organisation theory.

REFERENCES

Acker, J. (1990) 'Hierarchies, Jobs and Bodies: A Theory of Gendered Organizations', *Gender and Society*, 4 (2): 139–58

Acker, J. (1992) 'Gendering Organisational Theory', in Albert J. Mills and Peta Tancred (eds), *Gendering Organizational Analysis.* Newbury Park, CA: Sage, pp. 248–60

Acker, J. (2006) 'Inequality Regimes: Gender, Class and Race in Organizations', *Gender and Society*, 20 (4): 441–64

Adkins, L. (1995) *Gendered Work, Sexuality, Family and the Labour Market.* Buckingham: Open University Press

Adkins, L. and Lury, C. (1996) 'The Cultural, the Sexual, and the Gendering of the Labour Market', in Lisa Adkins and Vicki Merchant (eds), *Sexualising the Social: Power and the Organization of Sexuality.* Basingstoke: Macmillan, pp. 204–23

Ahmed, S. (2006) 'The Non-Performativity of Anti-Racism', *Merideans: Journal of Women, Race and Culture*, 7 (1): 104–26

Ahmed, S. (2007) '"You End up Doing the Document Rather than Doing the Doing": Race Equality, Diversity and the Politics of Documentation', *Ethnic and Racial Studies*, 30 (4): 590–609

Ahmed, S. and Swan, E. (2006) 'Introduction: Doing Diversity', Editorial of Special Issue of *Policy Futures in Education* on Doing Diversity in Education, 4 (2): 96–100

Ahmed, S., Hunter, S., Kilic, S., Swan, E. and Turner, L. (2006) *Integrating Diversity: Race, Gender and Leadership in the Learning and Skills Sector.* Final Report. Lancaster: Centre for Excellence in Leadership

Allen, B.J. (1995) '"Diversity" and Organisational Communication', *Journal of Applied Communication Research*, 23: 143–55

Alvesson, M. and Due Billing, Y. (1997) *Understanding Gender and Organizations.* London: Sage

Alvesson, M. and Due Billing, Y. (2002) 'Beyond Body-counting: A Discussion of the Social Construction of Gender at Work', in Iiris

Aaltio and Albert J. Mills (eds), *Gender, Identity and the Culture of Organizations*. London: Routledge, pp. 72–91

Association of University Teachers (2003) *The Unequal Academy, UK Academic Staff 1995–2003*. London: AUT

Back, L., Crabbe, T. and Solomos, J. (2001) *The Changing Face of Football: Racism, Identity and Multiculture in the English Game*. Oxford: Berg

Bagilhole, B. (1997) *Equal Opportunities and Social Policy*. London: Longman

Barnes, C. (2000) 'A Working Social Model? Disability, Work and Disability Politics in the 21st Century', *Critical Social Policy*, 20 (4): 441–57

Barrett, M. (1980/1988) *Women's Oppression Today: The Marxist/Feminist Encounter*. London: Verso

BBC News (2005) 'Pregnant? You're Fired!', http://news.bbc.co.uk 25/11/2005 (accessed on 25/11/2005)

Beasley, C. (1999) *What is Feminism? An Introduction to Feminist Theory*. London: Sage

Bell, E. and Nkomo, S. (2001) *Our Separate Ways: Black and White Women and the Struggle for Professional Identity*. Cambridge, MA: Harvard University Press

Benschop, Y. (2001) 'Pride, Prejudice and Performance', *International Journal of Human Resources Management*, 12 (7): 1166–81

Bernandes, J. (1997) *Family Studies: An Introduction*. London: Routledge

Bhavnani, R. (2001) *Rethinking Interventions in Racism*. Stoke on Trent: Commission for Racial Equality with Trentham Books

Birnie, J., Madge, C., Pain, R., Raghuram, P. and Rose, G. (2005) 'Working a Fraction and Making a Fraction Work: A Rough Guide for Geographers in the Academy', *Area*, 37 (3): 251–59

Blackmore, J. (2006) 'Social Justice and the Study and Practice of Leadership in Education: A Feminist History', *Journal of Educational Administration and History*, 38 (2): 185–200

Blair-Loy, M. (2003) *Competing Devotions: Career and Family among Women Executives*. Cambridge, MA: Harvard University Press

Brah, A. (1992) 'Difference, Diversity and Differentiation', in James Donald and Ali Rattansi (eds), *'Race', Culture and Difference*. London: Sage, pp. 126–45

Brah, A. (1996) *Cartographies of Diaspora: Contesting Identities*. London: Routledge

Brewis, J. and Linstead, S. (2004) 'Gender and Management', in S. Linstead, L. Fulop and S. Lilley (eds), *Management and Organization: A Critical Text*. Basingstoke: Palgrave Macmillan, pp. 56–92

Bruni, A. and Gherardi, S. (2002) 'Engendering Differences, Transgressing the Boundaries, Coping with the Dual Presence', in Iiris Aaltio and Albert J. Mills (eds), *Gender, Identity and the Culture of Organizations*. London: Routledge, pp. 21–38

Cabinet Office Strategy Unit (2003) *Ethnic Minorities and the Labour Market*. London: Strategy Unit, Cabinet Office

Carabine, J. (2004) 'Sexualities, Personal Lives and Social Policy', in Jean Carabine (ed.), *Sexualities*. Bristol: Policy Press with Open University Press, pp. 1–48

Chancer, L. and Watkins, B. (2006) *Gender, Race and Class: An Overview*. Oxford: Blackwell

Cockburn, C. (1989) 'Equal Opportunities: The Short and Long Agenda', *Industrial Relations Journal*, 20 (4): 213–25

Cockburn, C. (1991) *In the Way of Women: Men's Resistance to Sex Equality in Organisations*. Basingstoke: Macmillan

Cockburn, C. (2002) 'Resisting Equal Opportunities: The Issue of Maternity', in S. Jackson and S. Scott (eds), *Gender: A Sociological Reader*. London: Routledge, pp. 180–91

Colgan, F., Creegan, C., McKearney, A. and Wright, T. (2007) *Lesbian, Gay and Bisexual Workers: Equality, Diversity and Inclusion in the Workplace. A Qualitative Research Study*. London Metropolitan University: Comparative Organisations and Equality Research Centre

Collier, R. (1995) *Masculinity, Law and the Family*. London: Routledge

Collier, R. (2001) 'A Hard Time to be a Father? Reassessing the Relationship between Laws, Policy, and Family (Practices)', *Journal of Law and Society*, 28: 520–45

Collinson, D. and Collinson, M. (2004) 'The Power of Time: Leadership, Management and Gender', in C.F. Epstein and A.L. Kalleberg (eds), *Fighting for Time: Shifting the Boundaries of Work and Social life*. New York: Russell Sage Foundation, pp. 219–46

Connell, R.W. (1995) *Masculinities*. Cambridge: Polity Press

Cooper, D. (2004) *Challenging Diversity: Rethinking Equality and the Value of Difference*. Cambridge: Cambridge University Press.

Creed, W.E. Douglas (2006) 'Seven Conversations about the Same Thing: Homophobia and Heterosexism in the Workplace', in Alison M. Konrad, Pushkala Prasad and Judith K. Pringle (eds), *Handbook of Workplace Diversity*. London: Sage, pp. 371–40

Davidson, M.J. and Cooper, C.L. (1992) *Shattering the Glass Ceiling: The Woman Manager*. London: Paul Chapman

Davies, B. and Banks, C. (1992) 'The Gender Trap: A Feminist Poststructuralist Analysis of Primary School Children's Talk about Gender', *Journal of Curriculum Studies*, 24 (1): 1–25

Davis, K., Evans, M. and Lorber, J. (2006) *Handbook of Gender Studies*. London: Sage

Desmarais, S. and Alksnis, C. (2005) 'Gender Issues', in J. Barling, K. Kelloway and M. Frone (eds), *Handbook of Work Stress*. Thousand Oaks, CA: Sage, pp. 455–87

Dex, S., Joshi, H., Macran, S. and McCulloch, A. (1998) 'Women's Employment Transitions around Childbearing', *Oxford Bulletin of Economics and Statistics*, 60: 79

Dickens, L. (1994) 'The Business Case for Women's Equality: Is the Carrot Better than the Stick?', *Employee Relations*, 16 (8): 5–18

Dickens, L. (1999) 'Beyond the Business Case: A Three-pronged Approach to Equality Action', *Human Resource Management Journal*, 9 (1): 9–19

Disability Rights Commission (c. 2004) *Employing Disabled People: Top Tips for Small Businesses*. London: DRC

Duggan, L. (2003) *The Twilight of Equality: Neoliberalism, Cultural Politics and the Attack on Democracy*. Boston, MA: Beacon Press

Dunne, G. (1998) '"Pioneers behind Our Own Front Doors": Towards Greater Balance in the Organisation of Work in Partnerships', *Work, Employment and Society*, 12 (2): 273–95

Dunne, G. (2000) 'Lesbians as Authentic Workers? Institutional Heterosexuality and the Reproduction of Gender Inequalities', *Sexualities*, 3 (2): 133–48

Dunphy, R. (2000) *Sexual Politics: An Introduction*. Edinburgh: Edinburgh University Press

Dyhouse, C. (2006) *Students: A Gendered History*. London: Routledge

Eagly, A.H. and Karau, S.J. (2002) 'Role Congruity Theory of Prejudice toward Female Leaders', *Psychological Review*, 109 (3): 573–98

Economist, The (2005) 'Women in Business, the Conundrum of the Glass Ceiling', Special Report, *The Economist*, 23 July, 67–9

Edwards, P. and Wajcman, J. (2005) *The Politics of Working Life*. Oxford: Oxford University Press

EOC (2005a) *Sex and Power: Who Runs Britain*. Manchester: Equal Opportunities Commission

EOC (2005b) *Greater Expectations*. Manchester: Equal Opportunities Commission

Essed, P. (2005) 'Gendered Preferences in Racialized Spaces: Cloning the Physician', in Karim Murji and John Solomos (eds), *Racialization: Studies in Theory and Practice*. Oxford: Oxford University Press, pp. 228–47

Fawcett Society (2005) *Black and Minority Ethnic Women in the UK*. London: Fawcett Society

Ferreday, D. (2003) *Theories of Equality and Diversity: A Literature Review Working Paper*. Lancaster: Centre for Excellence in Leadership

Firestone, S. (1970) *The Dialectic of Sex*. New York: William Morrow and Co.

Fondas, N. and Sassalos, S. (2000) 'A Different Voice in the Boardroom: How the Presence of Women Directors Affects Board Influence over Management', *Global Focus*, 12 (2): 13–22

Fraser, N. (1997) *Justice Interruptus: Critical Reflections on the 'Postsocialist' Condition*. New York: Rouledge

Friedan, B. (1963) *The Feminine Mystique*. Harmondsworth: Penguin

Gatrell, C. (2005) *Hard Labour: The Sociology of Parenthood*. Maidenhead: Open University Press

Gatrell, C. (2007a) 'A Fractional Commitment?', *International Journal of Human Resource Management*, 18 (3): 462–75

Gatrell, C. (2007b) 'Secrets and Lies: Breastfeeding and Professional Paid Work', *Social Science and Medicine*, (65): 393–404

Gatrell, C. and Cooper, C.L. (2007) '(No) Cracks in the Glass Ceiling: Women Managers, Stress and the Barriers to Success', in D. Bilimoria and S. Piderit (eds), *Handbook on Women in Business and Management*. Cheltenham: Edward Elgar, pp. 57–77

Gewirtz, S., Ball, S.J. and Bowe, R. (1995) *Markets, Choice and Equity in Education*. London: Open University Press

Gherardi, S. (1995) *Gender, Symbolism and Organizational Cultures*. Newbury Park, CA: Sage

Giddens, A. (1984) *The Constitution of Society*. Cambridge: Polity Press

Ginn, J., Arber, S., Brannen, J., Dale, A., Dex, S., Elias, P., Moss, P., Pahl, J., Roberts, C. and Rubery, J. (1996) 'Feminist Fallacies: A Reply to Hakim on Women's Employment', *British Journal of Sociology*, 47: 167–74

Greer, G. (2006) *The Female Eunuch*. London: Harper Perennial (originally published in 1970)

Grint, K. (2005) *The Sociology of Work*. Cambridge: Polity Press

Hakim, C. (1995) 'Five feminist myths about women's employment', *British Journal of Sociology*, 46: 429–55

Hakim, C. (1996a) *Key Issues in Women's Work*. London: Athlone Press

Hakim, C. (1996b) 'The Sexual Division of Labour and Women's Heterogeneity', *British Journal of Sociology*, 47: 178–88

Hakim, C. (2000) *Work–Lifestyle Choices in the 21st Century: Preference Theory*. Oxford: Oxford University Press

Halford, S. and Leonard, P. (2001) *Gender, Power and Organisations*. Basingstoke: Palgrave

Hamilton, E. (2006) 'Whose Story Is It Anyway? Narrative Accounts of the Roles of Women in Founding and Establishing Family Businesses', *International Small Business Journal*, 23 (3): 1–16

Haywood, C. and Mac an Ghaill, M. (2003) *Men and Masculinities*. Buckingham: Open University Press

hooks, b. (1981) *Ain't I a Woman?* Boston: South End Press

hooks, b. (1986) 'Sisterhood, Political Solidarity between Women', *Feminist Review*, 23: 125–38

hooks, b. (1993) 'Lets get real about frminism the backlash, the myths, the movements', Interview in *Ms*, IV: 12

Höpfl, H. and Hornby Atkinson, P. (2000) 'The Future of Women's Careers', in A. Collin and R. Young (eds), *The Future of Career*. Cambridge: Cambridge University Press, pp. 130–43

Hoque, K. and Noon, M. (1999) 'Racial Discrimination in Speculative Applications: New Optimism Six Years On?', *Human Resource Management Journal*, 9 (3): 71–82

Horna, J. and Lupri, E. (1987) 'Father's Participation in Work, Family Life and Leisure: A Canadian Experience', in C. Lewis and M. O'Brien (eds), *Reassessing Fatherhood*. London: Sage, pp. 54–73

Howorth, C., Rose, M. and Hamilton, E. (2006) 'Definitions, Diversity and Development: Key Debates in Family Business Research', in M. Casson, B. Young and N. Wadeson (eds), *The Oxford Handbook of Entrepreneurship*. Oxford: Oxford University Press, pp. 225–47

Hughes, C. (2002) *Women's Contemporary Lives: Within and Beyond the Mirror*. London: Routledge

Humphrey, J.C. (1999) 'Organizing Sexualities, Organized Inequalities: Lesbians and Gay Men in Public Service Occupations', *Gender Work and Organization*, 6 (3): 134–51

Hunter, S. and Swan, E. (2007a) 'The Politics of Equality: Professionals, States and Activists', Editorial of Special Issue of *Equal Opportunities International* on The Politics of Equality: Professionals, States and Activists, 26 (5): 377–86

Hunter, S. and Swan, E. (2007b) 'Oscillating Politics and Shifting Agencies: Equalities and Diversity Work and Actor-Network Theory', in Special Issue of *Equal Opportunities International* on The Politics of Equality: Professionals, States and Activists, 26 (5): 402–19

Jackson, C., Furnham, A. and Willen, K. (2000) 'Employer Willingness to Comply with Disability Discrmination Act Regarding Staff Selection in the UK', *Journal of Occupational Psychology*, 73: 119–29

Jencks, C. (1998) 'Whom Must We Treat Equally for Educational Opportunity to be Equal?', *Ethics*, 98 (3): 518–33

Jewson, N. and Mason, D. (1986) 'The Theory and Practice of Equal Opportunities Policies: Liberal and Radical Approaches', *Sociological Review*, 34 (2): 307–34

Jewson, N. and Mason, D. (1994) 'Race, Employment and Equal Opportunities: Towards a Political Economy and Agenda for the 1990s', *Sociological Review*, 42 (4): 591–617

Johnson, W.B. and Packer, A.E. (1987) *Workforce 2000: Work and Workers for the 21st Century*. Indianapolis: Hudson Institute, Inc.

Jones, D. and Stablein, R. (2006) 'Diversity as Resistance and Recuperation: Critical Theory, Post-structural Perspectives and Workplace Diversity', in Alison Konrad, Pushkala Prasad and Judith Pringle (eds), *Handbook of Workplace Diversity*. London: Sage, pp. 145–66

Kandola, R. and Fullerton, J. (1994) *Managing the Mosaic: Diversity in Action*. London: Institute of Personnel and Development

Kerfoot, D. (2000) '"Body Work": Estrangement, Disembodiment and the Organizational "Other"', in J. Hassard, R. Holiday and H. Wilmott (eds), *Body and Organisation*. London: Sage, pp. 230–46

Kerfoot, D. and Knights, D. (1993) 'Management, Masculinity and Manipulation: From Paternalism to Corporate Strategy in Financial Services', *Journal of Management Studies*, 30 (4): 659–77

Kerfoot, D. and Knights, D. (1996) 'The Best is Yet to Come?: The Quest for Embodiment in Managerial Work', in D.L. Collinson and J. Hearn (eds), *Men as Managers, Managers and Men: Critical Perspectives on Men, Masculinities and Managements*. London: Sage, pp. 78–98

Kerr, J. (2005) *The Tiger Who Came to Tea*. London: HarperCollins Publishers Ltd, originally published by William Collins and Co. in 1968

Kirton, G. and Greene, A.-M. (2000) *The Dynamics of Managing Diversity*. London: Heinemann

Kirton, G. and Greene, A.-M. (2004) *The Dynamics of Managing Diversity: A Critical Approach*. Second edition. Oxford: Elsevier-Butterworth-Heinemann

Konrad, A.M., Prasad, P. and Pringle, J.K. (eds) (2006) *Handbook of Workplace Diversity*. London: Sage

Kothari, U. (2005) 'Authority and Expertise: The Professionalization of International Development and the Ordering of Dissent', in Nina Laurie and Liz Bondi (eds), *Working the Spaces of Neoliberalism*. Oxford: Blackwell, pp. 32–53

Lent, A. (2001) *British Social Movements since 1945: Sex, Colour, Peace and Power*. Basingstoke: Palgrave

Lewis, G. (2000) *'Race', Gender and Social Welfare: Encounters in a Postcolonial Society*. Cambridge: Polity Press

Lewis, S. (2006) *Gender Parenthood and the Changing European Workplace*. Final Report of the Fifth Framework Project. Brussels: European Commission

Liff, S. (1999) 'Diversity and Equal Opportunities: Room for a Constructive Compromise?', *Human Resource Management Journal*, 9 (1): 65–75

Lingard, B., Hayes, D., Mills, M. and Christie, P. (2003) *Leading Learning: Making Hope Practical in Schools*. Maidenhead: Open University Press

Litvin, D.R. (1997) 'The Discourse of Diversity: From Biology to Management', *Organization*, 4 (2): 187–209

Litvin, D.R. (2002) 'The Business Case for Diversity and the "Iron Cage"', in Barbara Czarniawska and Heather Hopfl (eds), *Casting the Other: The Production and Maintenance of Inequalities in Work Organizations*. London: Routledge, pp. 160–84

Longhurst, R. (2001) *Bodies: Exploring Fluid Boundaries*. London: Routledge

Lorbiecki, A. (2001) 'Changing Views on Diversity Management: The Rise of the Learning Perspective and the Need to Recognise Social and Political Contradictions', *Management Learning*, 32 (3): 345–61

Lorbiecki, A. and Jack, G. (2000) 'Critical Turns in the Evolution of Diversity Management', *British Journal of Management*, Special Issue, 11: 17–31

Lowery, M. (1995) 'The War on Equal Opportunity', *Black Enterprise*, 25: 1–5

Mac an Ghaill, M. (1999) *Contemporary Racisms and Ethnicities: Social and Cultural Transformations*. Buckingham: Open University Press

Macpherson, W. (1999) *The Stephen Lawrence Inquiry*. London: Home Office

McDowell, L. (1999) *Gender, Identity and Place*. Cambridge: Polity Press

McRae, S. (2003) 'Choice and Constraints in Mothers' Employment Careers: McRae replies to Hakim', *British Journal of Sociology*, 54 (4): 585–92

Maddock, S. (1999) *Challenging Women: Gender, Culture and Organization*. London: Sage

Malthouse, T.-J. (1997) *Childcare, Business and Social Change*. London: Institute of Directors

Marshall, A. (1994) 'Sensuous Sapphires: A Study of the Social Construction of Black Female Sexuality', in M. Maynard and J. Purvis (eds), *Researching Women's Lives from a Feminist Perspective*. London: Taylor & Francis, pp. 106–211

Martin, E. (1992) *The Woman in the Body: A Cultural Analysis of Reproduction*. Boston, MA: Beacon Press

Mills, A. and Tancred, P. (1992) *Gendering Organizational Analysis*. Newbury Park, CA: Sage

Mills, E. (2007) 'It Beats the Hell Out of a Nursery', *The Sunday Times*, News Review, 8 April: 4

Mir, R., Mir, A. and Wong, D.J. (2006) 'Diversity: The Cultural Logic of Global Capital?', in A.M. Konrad, P. Prasad and J.K. Pringle (eds), *Handbook of Workplace Diversity*. London: Sage, pp. 167–87

Mogdan, G. (2005) 'Depoliticizing Diversity in US Public Discourse', paper presented at 9th International Pragmatics Conference, Riva del Garda, Italy, 10–15 July

Moi, T. (2005) *Sex, Gender and the Body: The Student Edition of What is a Woman*. Oxford: Oxford University Press

Monro, S. (2007) 'New Institutionalism and Sexuality at Work in Local Government', *Gender, Work and Organization*, 14 (1): 1–19

Morris, L. (1990) *The Workings of the Household*. Cambridge: Polity Press

Mulholland, K. (1996) 'Gender, Power and Property Relations within Enterpreneurial Wealthy Families', *Gender Work and Organisation*, 3 (2): 78–102

Murji, K. and Solomos, J. (2005) 'Introduction', in Karim Murji and John Solomos (eds), *Racialization: Studies in Theory and Practice*. Oxford: Oxford University Press, pp. 1–28

Nast, H. and Pile, S. (eds) (1998) *Places Through the Body*. London: Routledge

Nelson, D.L. and Quick, J.C. (1985) 'Professional Women: Are Distress and Disease Inevitable?', *Academy of Management Review*, 10: 206–18

Oakley, A. (1981) *From Here to Maternity: Becoming a Mother*. Harmondsworth: Penguin (Pelican Books)

Oakley, A. (1984) *The Captured Womb*. Oxford: Blackwell

Oerton, S. (1996) 'Sexualizing the Organization, Lesbianizing the Women: Gender, Sexuality and "Flat" Organizations', *Gender, Work and Organization*, 3 (1): 25–37

Omanovic, V. (2006) *A Production of Diversity: Appearances, Ideas, Interests, Actions, Contradictions and Praxis*. Gotenburg: BAS Publishing

Omi, M. and Winant, H. (1986) *Racial Formation in the United States: From the 1960s to the 1980s*. New York: Routledge

Padavic, I. and Reskin, B. (2002) *Women and Men at Work*. Thousand Oaks, CA: Sage

Parsons, T. and Bales, R. (1956) *Family and Socialization and Interaction Process*. London: Routledge and Kegan Paul

Penketh, L. (2000) *Tackling Institutional Racism: Anti-racist Policies and Social Work Education and Training*. Bristol: Policy Press

Porter, S. (1998) *Social Theory and Nursing Practice*. London: Macmillan

Prasad, P. and Mills, A. (1997) 'From Showcase to Shadow: Understanding the Dilemmas of Managing Workplace Diversity', in Pushkala Prasad, Albert J. Mills, Michael Elmes and Anshuman Prasad (eds), *Managing the Organizational Melting Pot: Dilemmas of Workplace Diversity*. Thousand Oaks, CA: Sage, pp. 3–30

Prasad, P., Mills, A., Elmes, M. and Prasad, A. (eds) (1997) *Managing the Organizational Melting Pot*. London: Sage

Pringle, R. (1989) *Secretaries Talk: Sexuality, Power and Work*. London: Verso

Pringle, R. (1998) *Sex and Medicine*. Cambridge: Cambridge University Press

Proudford, K. and Nkomo, S. (2006) 'Race and Ethnicity in Organizations', in Alison M. Konrad, Pushkala Prasad and Judith K. Pringle (eds), *Handbook of Workplace Diversity*. London: Sage

Puwar, N. (2004) *Space Invaders: Race, Gender and Bodies Out of Place*. Oxford: Berg

Ramsay, K. and Letherby, G. (2006) 'The Experience of Academic Non-mothers in the Gendered University', *Gender Work and Organisation*, 13 (1): 25–44

Rattansi, A. (1992) 'Introduction', in James Donald and Ali Rattansi (eds), *'Race', Culture and Difference*. London: Sage, pp. 1–10

Rattansi, A. (2005) 'The Uses of Racialization: The Time–Spaces and Subject–Objects of the Raced Body', in Karim Murji and John Solomos (eds), *Racialization: Studies in Theory and Practice*. Oxford: Oxford University Press, pp. 271–86

Rich, A. (1977) *Of Woman Born: Motherhood as Experience and Institution*. London: Virago

Richards, W. (2001) 'Evaluating Equal Opportunities Initiatives: The Case for a "Transformative" Agenda', in M. Noon and E. Ogbonna (eds), *Equality, Diversity and Disadvantage in Employment*. London: Macmillan, pp. 15–31

Rowbotham, S. (1997) *A Century of Women: The History of Women in Britain and the United States*. London: Penguin

Runnymede Trust (2006) *Why Preferential Policies Can Be Fair*. London: Runnymede Trust

Scraton, S. (1990) *Gender and Physical Education*. Melbourne, Vic.: Deakin University Press

Seager, J. (2005) *The Atlas of Women in the World*. London: Earthscan

Showalter, E. and Showalter, E. (1972) 'Victorian Women and Menstruation', in M. Vicinus (ed.), *Suffer and Be Still: Women in the Victorian Age*. London: Indiana University Press, pp. 38–44

Singh, V. and Vinnicombe, S. (2004) 'Why So Few Women Directors in Top UK Boardrooms? Evidence and Theoretical Explanations', *Corporate Governance*, 12 (4): 479–88

Squires, J. (2003) *Equality and Diversity: A New Equality Framework for Britain?* London: School of Public Policy, University College London

Summerfield, P. (1998) *Reconstructing Women's Wartime Lives*. Manchester: Manchester University Press

Swain, J., French, S. and Cameron, C. (2003) *Controversial Issues in a Disabling Society*. Buckingham: Open University Press

Swan, E. (2005) 'On Bodies, Rhinestones and Pleasures: Women Teaching Managers', *Management Learning*, 36 (3): 317–33

Swan, E. and Hunter, S. (2007) 'Fixing Diversity: Diversity Management, Boundary Objects, and Travelling Companions', Paper under review for *Scandinavian Journal of Management*, Special Issue on Diversity Management? Translation? Travel?

Thomas, C. (2007) *Female Forms: Experiencing and Understanding Disability*. Maidenhead: Open University Press

Thomas, R. (1990) 'From Affirmative Action to Affirming Diversity', *Harvard Business Review*, 90 (2): 107–12

Tooley, J. (2002) *The Miseducation of Women*. London: Continuum

Treanor, J. (2006) 'No Room at the Top: Fewer Women Reaching Boards of Britain's Top Firms', *The Guardian*, 8 November: 3

Truman, C. (1996) 'Paid Work in Women's Lives: Continuity and Change', in T. Cosslett, A. Easton and P. Summerfield (eds), *Women, Power and Resistance: An Introduction to Women's Studies*. Buckingham: Open University Press, pp. 35–47

TUC (1999) *Straight Up! Why the Law Should Protect Lesbian and Gay Workers*. London: TUC

Tyler, I. (2000) 'Reframing Pregnant Embodiment', in S. Ahmed, J. Kilby, S. Lury, M. McNeil and B. Skeggs (eds), *Transformations: Thinking Through Feminism*. London: Routledge, pp. 288–302

Unison (2003) Unpublished Survey of Unison LGBT Members. London: Unison

US Department of Labor (2005) *Employment Status of Women and Men in 2005*, http://www.dol.gov/wb/factsheets (accessed 23/08/2006)

Valeska, L. (1975) 'If All Else Fails I'm Still a Mother', in J. Treblicot (ed.) (1984), *Mothering: Essays in Feminist Theory*. Lanham, MD: Savage, Rowman and Littlefield, pp. 70–80

Vinnicombe, S. and Bank, J. (2003) *Women with Attitude: Lessons for Career Management*. London: Routledge

Wajcman, J. (1998) *Managing Like a Man: Women and Men in Corporate Management*. Cambridge: Polity Press

Walby, S. (1990) *Theorising Patriarchy*. Oxford: Blackwell

Walker, H. (2002) *A Genealogy of Equality: The Curriculum for Social Work Education and Training*. London: Woburn

Warner, M. (1999) *The Trouble with Normal: Sex, Politics, and the Ethics of Queer Life*. New York: Free Press

West, C. and Zimmerman, D. (1987) 'Doing Gender', *Gender and Society*, 1 (2): 125–51

Wharton, A. (2005) *The Sociology of Gender: An Introduction to Theory and Research*. Malden, MA: Blackwell

Whitehead, S. (2002) *Men and Masculinities*. Cambridge: Polity Press

Wiegman, R. (2000) 'On Being Married to the Institution', in Shirley Geok-lin Lim and Maria Herrera-Sobek (eds), *Power, 'Race' and Gender in Academe*. New York: Modern Language Association, pp. 71–82

Williams, J. (1999) *Unbending Gender: Why Work and Family Conflict and What To Do About It*. New York: Oxford University Press

Williams, J.C. and Cohen Cooper, H. (2005) 'The Public Policy of Motherhood', in M. Biernat, F. Crosby and J.C. Williams (eds), 'The Maternal Wall: Research and Policy Perspectives on Discrimination Against Mothers', *Journal of Social Issues*, 60 (4): 849–65

Wilson, E. and Iles, P. (1996) 'Managing Diversity: Evaluation of an Emerging Paradigm', Proceedings of British Academy Annual Conference September 1996, Aston Business School, pp. 6.62–6.76

Wollstonecraft, M. (2004) *A Vindication of the Rights of Woman*. London: Penguin (originally published 1792)

Women and Work Commission (2006) *Shaping a Fairer Future*. London: Department of Communities and Local Government

Woodhams, C. and Corby, S. (2003) 'Defining Disability in Theory and Practice: A Critique of the British Disability Discrimination Act 1995', *Journal of Social Policy*, 32 (2): 159–78

Young, I.M. (2005) *On Female Body Experience: Throwing Like a Girl and other Essays*. Oxford: Oxford University Press

INDEX